Jing

Look forward to working with you on your asset protection.

ASSET PROTECTION

FOR REAL ESTATE INVESTORS

# ASSET PROTECTION
## for Real Estate Investors

Clint Coons

Anderson Law Group
*www.andersonadvisors.com*

Copyright 2009 by Clint M. Coons
Published by: Alabaster Financial, LLC
3225 McLeod Drive #100
Las Vegas, NV 89121
Telephone: 702.871.8535

All rights reserved. No part of this publication may be reproduced or transmitted in any form or by any means, electronic or mechanical, including photocopy, recording or any information storage and retrieval system now known or to be invented, without permission in writing from the publisher, except by a reviewer who wishes to quote brief passages in connection with a review for inclusion in a magazine, newspaper, or broadcast. Requests for permission should be addressed in writing to the publisher. This book is designed to provide accurate and authoritative information on the subject of asset protection. While all of the cases and examples described in the book are loosely based on experiences, most of the names and situations have been changed to protect privacy. It is sold with the understanding that neither the author nor the publisher is engaged in rendering legal, accounting, financial, or other professional advice. As each individual situation is unique, questions specific to your circumstances should be addressed to an appropriate professional to ensure that your situation has been evaluated carefully and appropriately. The author and the publisher specifically disclaim any liability or loss incurred as a consequence, directly or indirectly, of using and applying any of the concepts in this book.

Printed in the United States of America

Paperback
ISBN: 978-0-9797860-1-3

Hardback
ISBN: 978-0-9797860-2-0

LCCN: 2009909798

Cover image: Author image by Studio3.com. Lock image iStockphoto©andynwt
Book design and page formatting by DesignForBooks.com

Edited by Kristin A. Cohen

# Contents

ACKNOWLEDGEMENT ............................................................. IX

INTRODUCTION TO ASSET PROTECTION
—ARE YOU REALLY AT RISK? ................................................ 1

Liability and Litigation ............................................................. 5
Forms of Liability .................................................................... 7
Know Your Enemy ................................................................. 11
Types of Liens ....................................................................... 12
Protecting Yourself ................................................................ 13

**1** BARRIERS TO ASSET PROTECTION—DO IT RIGHT OR
DON'T DO IT AT ALL ......................................................... 15

The Uniform Fraudulent Transfers Act (UFTA) ......................... 17
Issues For Determining Fraudulent Transfers ........................... 18
Bankruptcy ........................................................................... 22

**2** EXEMPT ASSETS—NO SENSE IN PROTECTING
WHAT IS ALREADY PROTECTED ......................................... 29

Homestead ........................................................................... 30
IRAs and Pension Plans ......................................................... 34
Annuities ............................................................................. 37
Life Insurance ...................................................................... 39

*www.andersonadvisors.com*

**3** ANONYMITY IN ASSET PROTECTION PLANNING
—APPEAR TO QUALIFY FOR FOOD STAMPS ..................... 43

Equity Stripping ................................................................. 46
Home Equity Line of Credit .............................................. 48
Second Mortgages on Rental Properties ............................ 50
Friendly Liens and Controlled Equity Stripping ............... 52

**4** LAND TRUSTS—PRIVACY PLUS PROTECTION
EQUALS PROFIT ...................................................... 59

Constructing a Land Trust ................................................ 62
Why Investors Use Land Trusts ........................................ 67
Situations Where an Investor Should Avoid Using a Land Trust ....... 69
Issues with Land Trusts ..................................................... 74

**5** COMPARISON OF BUSINESS ENTITIES—STRIKING A BALANCE
BETWEEN ASSET PROTECTION AND TAXATION .................. 77

Liability Protection ........................................................... 77
The Corporation ............................................................... 79
Limited Partnership .......................................................... 81
Limited Liability Company .............................................. 85
Series Limited Liability Company .................................... 89
Trusts ................................................................................ 90
Nevada, Delaware, Wyoming—The Organizers Dilemma ............... 93

**6** ASSET PROTECTION FOR REAL ESTATE
—INSURANCE IS NOT YOUR ONLY OPTION ..................... 99

Investment Objectives: Long-Term Deals .......................... 101
Charging Order Protections .............................................. 104

Charging Order Problems .................................................................. 106
Real Estate Taxation and LLCs ......................................................... 108
One LLC for Every Property ............................................................. 111
Partnering with Others on Real Estate Investments ......................... 113
Where Should Your LLC Be Organized? ......................................... 114

# 7    Short-Term Investing—Quick turns, Wholesaling and Other Strategies ....................... 117

Know What Makes a Dealer and Plan Accordingly.......................... 121
Avoiding Dealer Status ...................................................................... 123
Where Should You Incorporate? ....................................................... 127

# 8    IRAs and Real Estate ............................................. 133

Steps To Acquiring Real Estate in an IRA ........................................ 140
Enhanced Control and Asset Protection for Your IRA .................... 141

# 9    Case Studies ............................................................ 145

Case Study 1 ...................................................................................... 145
Case Study 2 ...................................................................................... 147
Case Study 3 ...................................................................................... 150
Case Study 4 ...................................................................................... 153
Case Study 5 ...................................................................................... 156
Case Study 6 ...................................................................................... 159

Appendix A: Homestead Laws ........................................................... 161
Appendix B: Overview of State LLC Asset
    Protection Laws............................................................................ 167

# Acknowledgement

I would like to begin by thanking my dad and mom for the work ethic they instilled in me as a child. Although at the time I could not see the future personal benefit of spending many weekends working for my father on his various real estate holdings, I did learn some important life lessons: tackle every job as if you are the owner and opportunity is created through hard work. These life lessons have carried me through my career and serve as a reminder that anything can be accomplished if one is determined.

Also, I would also like to recognize my wife of 17 years, Tracy, who gave me two wonderful children, Carter and Carly. Her patience while this book was being written as well as her willingness to read my multiple drafts and offer constructive criticism proved invaluable in bringing this work to completion.

# Introduction to Asset Protection—
*Are You Really at Risk?*

**W**ho are you? Chances are if you've picked up this book, you're an investor who is a lot like one of these people:

Amy, a retired social worker living on a fixed income, has decided to use her savings to buy a roadside motel in another state. After a mild stroke, she's hired a manager to take charge of the largely short-term renters. That way, she hopes to spend less time and effort managing her property and more time with her grandkids.

Barry is a family man with two jobs renting out a waterfront condominium. Because of its proximity to the ocean, the house is a hot party spot, sometimes resulting in a big mess to clean up. Luckily, Barry has two teenage sons who pitch in to care for the property, and to throw out junk left by tenants who skip out on the rent.

Clara, a doctor who bought a run-down brownstone in a now-trendy neighborhood, is planning to renovate and live on the top floor. Her accountant mentioned that the building has some mold, but since no tenants have complained so far, Clara figures it's no big deal. Most of them were pretty understanding about the rent hike for the renovations.

What do these three people have in common? They are hardworking people who have scrimped and saved, with coupons and penny counting, to acquire enough money to invest for their future. By investing in real estate, they believe their money is safe and, better yet, profitable. They all feel pretty confident in their financial and investment planning decisions. They are not out to conquer the world or become the next Donald Trump—they would just like to see a healthy, consistent profit out of their investment. Like all of us, what they most want is financial security.

Instead, they are going to get lawsuits. Lots of them. Why?

The manager Amy hired to run her motel drinks on the job and invites his friends over. They get into a fight with some of the renters. In the heat of the scuffle, Amy's manager pulls out a gun and fires, seriously wounding a renter. The police arrest Amy's manager, but it is Amy who has to face the lawsuits from the injured renter, who wants millions of dollars because he'll never walk again.

When the latest band of partiers abandons the place prematurely, Barry waits 60 days, and then goes in with his sons to clean up the place for the next renter. One month later, his absentee tenants have filed a lawsuit, claiming that Barry threw out valuable art and furniture worth more than $10,000. Barry knows that all that was left was junk, not valuable art, but he can't prove it since he threw everything out a long time ago.

Clara's renovations go well, and things are fine for a year, until one of the neighbor's kids gets asthma. His mother brings in specialists and building inspectors to look at building, and they conclude that the mold has contributed to the asthma. Not only is Clara stuck with the costs of bringing the building up to code, but she also faces a lawsuit from anyone who developed asthma in her brownstone. Suddenly her chic investment is a nightmare.

These situations may sound dramatic, but they're not. As a businessman, attorney, and real estate investor, I have encountered these situations time and again. Clients who rely on luck and goodwill to keep their money safe are going to be in for a nasty shock. Even common sense can't help in asset planning these days. You need solid financial planning to safeguard your investments against litigation. And the time is now; the number of lawsuits in America is growing exponentially, with neighbor more than willing to sue neighbor.

And it's getting worse. Every day, more than 20,000 lawsuits are filed in America, totaling more than $80,000,000 a year. Most of these lawsuits are settled out of court in expensive, humiliating settlements that can lead to bankruptcy, or worse. It is estimated that nearly three out of every four lawyers in the world practices in the United States, and competition for cases—or to create a case where there is none—is ferocious. One thing is always certain: When you have money, you become a target for lawsuits. Here's one example. Damages—the amount in question in a civil lawsuit—are calculated as including both compensatory (what was actually suffered) and punitive (to punish the wrongdoer, so he doesn't do it again). Punitive damages are often dependent on how much money is in the wrongdoer's bank account—which is why McDonald's gets

*For a comprehensive overview of lawsuit abuse in America check out www.facesoflawsuitabuse.org.*

sued for billions over one overheated cup of coffee. The more money you have, the more you risk being a defendant in a lawsuit. With lawyers working on contingency fees and holding classes for potential clients on how to bring lawsuits, this risk grows every day.

This is where asset protection comes in—to ward off the never-ending threat of litigation, and to keep your money where it belongs: in your pocket. After all, there's no point in saving and investing your money if it leaves you wide open and unprotected from frivolous (and expensive) legal action. Asset protection involves both pre-litigation planning and risk management—a way to protect your hard-earned wealth and to make it work *for you*, not *against you*. In the above examples, Amy, Barry, and Clara didn't go looking for trouble, and they certainly didn't deserve what they got. But if they had taken a few cautionary steps at the beginning of their investment, they could have protected their nest eggs.

What's going to happen to these investors?

> Amy's savings account can be seized to pay the damages in the lawsuit.
>
> Barry might need a second mortgage on the house to replace his renters' belongings—or at least, what his renters claimed were their belongings.
>
> Clara has to spend her own time and money trying to get the previous owner of the brownstone to pay her for the costs of all the repairs, but finds that there aren't any laws in place to help her.

Asset protection always boils down one thing: minimizing liabilities. A liability is the exact opposite of an asset—something that can work against you, rather than for you. It can be a weakness in your financial planning that allows others access to your savings, or it can be a broken railing in the stairwell of one of your rental buildings. A liability, in short, is a financial weakness. A good asset protection planner will reduce the liabilities that you face, simply because you saved your money and invested it wisely. What many people forget is that there are many, many forms of liability. While you're making sure that your yearly taxes stay low, you may still be leaving yourself wide open for a civil lawsuit. And if you're found liable in a civil suit, everything you own personally will be at risk.

In particular, real estate investors need solid advice and guidance because the liabilities that accompany real estate ownership are unique and often complicated, and they can result in enormous sums of money going out the door. Many of those who try to "go it alone" with their financial planning—or, even worse, depend on the advice of friends and family—end up in serious trouble. Your loved ones may have your best interests at heart, but they can't prepare you for the jungle of tax liabilities and potential litigation that you'll face once you invest in any type of real estate.

## LIABILITY AND LITIGATION

At Anderson Business Advisors, we have two main goals for asset protection: Keep your taxes low, and protect your money from unscrupulous litigants. Many real estate investors rely on an attorney or a financial advisor to put together this plan, but that simply doesn't work. Why? The answer is simple: Either they lack the knowledge, or they don't value your assets.

With many attorneys, you must have millions of dollars in assets before anything other than insurance is recommended to you. I often ask my clients: "If I took $100,000 from you, would it hurt?" The answer is "Yes" 100% of the time. It is this understanding of my clients' value systems and what insurance will or will not cover in a lawsuit that brings thousands of people to my workshops and law firm each year to protect their assets. For example, I recently had a conversation with my client's CPA, whom we will call "Jim." Jim was questioning why I created an LLC for my client's $250,000 brokerage account. I explained the concept of asset protection and how our joint client, a dentist, could lose his assets in the event of a lawsuit. The CPA remained unconvinced. Unfortunately, this is typical. Jim told me he has several dentists as clients and that not one had been sued. So in Jim's opinion, because it hasn't happened yet means that it won't. Wow. Playing the "I won't get sued game" is like not buying auto insurance because you have never been in a wreck. Just because it hasn't happened doesn't mean it never will.

*Want a more detailed understanding of Asset Protection and the threats you face individually? Go to www.andersonadvisors.com and register for a free Gold membership. If you are a first time user, then go to our Products section and search for "Understanding Asset Protection Planning kit." The kit is FREE and it includes a complimentary one hour consultation.*

A good asset protection planner has the skills of both an attorney and a CPA, as well as a deeper understanding of your goals and your priorities. In my case, I know I understand the perspective of a real estate investor, because I am one. So was my father—he's "Barry" from the above example, and I was the son helping him manage his property. I remember his frustration as he was cited for breaking laws he never knew about, laws that always seemed to favor the tenant. My brother and I would clean out rental properties to keep them in habitable condition, only to watch them get trashed by thoughtless renters. When faced with a lawsuit about the "valuable art" he threw out, my father realized that common sense worked against him, rather than for him. Watching him struggle made me even more determined to help people like him—ordinary investors who didn't understand the quirks and roadblocks involved in the simple act of buying and renting out a property.

## FORMS OF LIABILITY

If you want your assets to be protected, you need to understand the various forms of liability out there. This is a complicated area, and you should definitely get help from a professional about which liabilities are relevant to your situation, but, just so you get an idea, here's an outline.

First, there are liabilities that affect you or the immediate members of your family. As the head of the family, you are responsible for all the minors and pets under your roof. For the most part, these types of liabilities aren't what we're discussing here, simply because they don't involve an investment of money. They come up in emergency situations—for example, if your dog bites a neighbor, or your son goes joyriding. You can't always predict them, and they're not always severe.

But real estate investors are entering a new world full of liabilities and high financial risk. Property ownership is almost always publicly recorded, which means that anyone can figure out what you're worth, and what your financial weaknesses are. If you don't maintain the property and keep it up to code, you're going to be liable for any accidents that happen on your land. If you make too much noise, you can be considered a nuisance and be fined. If your neighbor doesn't like the leaves from your tree blowing into his backyard, he can make you pay for the cleanup. Anything that's attractive to kids—a duck pond, a swimming pool, a snowmobile—needs to be locked up and only available to kids under your supervision. If they get hurt, guess who'll end up paying the medical bills? That's right, you—even if you had a "no trespassing" sign up.

If your renters are arrested for dealing drugs out of an apartment you rent to them, you could be liable if the cops think you knew about it. You are liable if your building or complex has any dangers or hazards: a loose railing in the stairwell, an elevator call button that doesn't work, or a doorman who sleeps on the job. All of these are liabilities you face as a property owner and landlord. The list goes on and on.

If you are a sole proprietor who is running your business yourself, in your name, then you're wide open to lawsuits and excessive taxes. If you organize, operate, and file as a corporation or a limited liability company, then you face a whole different set of financial liabilities. We'll discuss the different types of business entities later in the book. All you need to know is that business in 21st century America is no longer a matter of buying a shop and putting out your shingle. It's complicated, and you'll need solid legal and tax planning, as well as a good idea of what your specific risks and liabilities are. It's only with the whole set of planning in all areas—tax, law, and property management—that your assets are truly protected. Not all asset protection firms cover all the bases, but here at Anderson Business Advisors, we make sure you're protected from every angle.

Without describing the different corporate entities yet (we'll do that later), let's take a look at the two main liability issues that every real estate investor needs to know about:

### Inside liability

In the case of inside liability, the entity (corporation, limited liability company (LLC), etc.) is held responsible and liable, but the owners of the entity are not. Let's say Ernie owns a corporation, and Frank is on the board of directors that runs the corporation. Ernie doesn't have to worry about inside liability, but Frank, who is responsible for the corporation does.

**Outside liability**
As you might guess, this is the same thing, only in reverse. In this case, if the owner of the entity is sued for anything—whether it's stock fraud or a hit-and-run—the assets of the LLC are safe, and separate from personal assets. So, if Ernie created an LLC to manage his rental properties, then the assets of the LLC are safe in case he's found liable in a personal lawsuit.

For the average person, all this talk about different types of liability is confusing. Does the average real estate investor really have to know about all this stuff? The answer is yes and no. No, you don't have to be familiar with all the technical issues of liability, but, yes, your advisor does. Otherwise, you'll learn all about liability the wrong way—in court.

For now, just remember this: For your asset protection plan to work, you need to be protected from inside and outside liability. In the above example, Ernie's money is safe because his asset specialist knew where the dangers lurked and set up a secure system in case of trouble. That's what I can do for you.

Protection from inside and outside liability in lawsuits, and protection from the IRS is the cornerstone of a solid asset protection program. You can navigate the complicated waters of real estate investing if you have the right guides to help you out—and if you know what you should look out for. Otherwise, if a court determines that you owe money, almost any asset under your name can be seized to pay your debts. They'll leave you with just enough money to support your family, but after that, you'll be on your own with rebuilding your financial future, and probably worse for wear.

Maybe you don't have many debts now, but that's unlikely if you live in today's America. The reality is that everyone is a debtor, or debt-ower, to a creditor some time in their life. The creditor can be your Aunt Sally or Uncle Sam, or any number of organizations willing to lend money to you—at a price. Creditors are interested in one thing: getting a return on the money they lent you.

You can become a debtor voluntarily, by borrowing money, or involuntarily.

> Frank is careful with his retirement savings, but he decides to invest in some commercial property in downtown Tampa. He goes to a bank and gets a mortgage, and therefore becomes a debtor voluntarily. However, after Gena's beauty salon takes up residence in the first floor of Frank's building, an inspector finds that the electrical wiring is not up to code. Frank is suddenly hit with fines and the costs of fixing the wiring, and because Gena can't use the space, she wants her money back for the months she paid in advance. Because he doesn't have the funds and can't borrow any more money, Frank is forced to file for bankruptcy. Frank has suddenly become involuntarily in debt—to government, to his handyman, and to Gena. And because he didn't plan ahead and kept his retirement savings in a non-qualified retirement account, e.g., IRA, he might have to dip into that money to satisfy his new debts.

You can avoid voluntary debt simply enough: Don't borrow money! But that's not always practical. And it's much harder to avoid involuntary debt, simply because, by definition, you don't see it coming. If there's a core belief that all good asset protection is built around, it's Murphy's Law: Anything that can go wrong will go wrong. At first it may sound pessimistic, but anticipating trouble early in the game helps you considerably reduce the risk of involuntary debt.

To understand asset protection, you need to understand how your assets are vulnerable to financial predators. You need to understand how creditors think and operate, as well as how they can obtain an "interest" in your property. In short, to quote Sun Tzu in *The Art of War*:

## KNOW YOUR ENEMY

Creditors come in two types:

- **Unsecured:** The creditor has a claim against the debtor, but not a claim over one particular asset or property of the debtor. Credit cards and some business lines of credit are usually unsecured loans.
- **Secured:** The creditor can lay claim to a particular asset, and if the debt isn't paid, the courts can seize the asset and transfer it to the creditor. Mortgages and credit used to buy a particular property—for example, a laptop computer—are secured debts.

A secured creditor is clearly more dangerous to the real estate investor—especially if that creditor can lay claim to the real estate in question! The interest a secured creditor has in the debtor's property is known as a **lien.** Liens are never good news, but some liens are especially bad for the investor looking to protect his assets and real property. The most common types of liens are listed on the next page.

## TYPES OF LIENS

1. **Consensual Liens:** You asked for it, you got it. Consensual liens include all the bank loans you received to buy property, or when you put up property in a mortgage to get more cash. These types of loans aren't too bad, as most of the time the debtor keeps control over the property and isn't required to hand it over to the creditor to get the money in the first place, this is typically referred to as a "deed of trust". However, in some cases, whether you're borrowing to purchase something (a purchase-money security interest lien) or putting up your property to get more money (a non-purchase-money security interest lien), the creditor will take ownership of the property in question up front in the form of a mortgage. A mortgage, unlike a deed of trust, gives the lender legal title to the property until the debt is paid off.

2. **Statutory Liens:** Speaking of federal and state laws, here's how they can work against you. There are certain types of liens that are secured by law, such as tax liens from the government for unpaid taxes. There are also mechanic's liens that arise when you don't pay the mechanic working on your car, or the contractor working on your house. There's not too much you can do about statutory liens once they're in place against you, but you can still figure out the best way to avoid them in the first place.

3. **Judgment Liens:** These are the bogeymen of the asset protection world. Judgment liens arise when a court issues a judgment that grants the creditor a lien on the debtor's property. This is what happens when someone files a civil suit against you, and the jury finds that you're liable. The person who filed the suit is the plaintiff, and once they've won, they're the "judgment creditor." A judgment creditor can levy on

your house, vehicle, and bank accounts. Your wages could be garnished, your bank account could be emptied, or your car could be seized and sold—all to satisfy your debt to your judgment creditor. However, with the proper structure in place, these assets can be protected.

## PROTECTING YOURSELF

By now the world looks pretty grim. Trust me, it can get worse, since there are many, many threats to your assets that I haven't told you about. But let me answer the question that's probably on your mind: What can I do about all those liabilities and liens? Well, you can't eliminate them all, but you can reduce the risk they present to your assets and financial security.

Most consensual and statutory liens can't be eliminated, even when they're attached to protected, or exempt, assets. Exempt assets are defined by states in their laws, and they can vary wildly. Sometimes business partnership property is exempt. Most of the time alimony and child support are exempt. Medical equipment, Bibles, schoolbooks, and burial plots are all exempt. Exemptions vary from state to state, but a good asset planner will have a reference guide to make sure you're getting the most exempt assets for your state. We'll get more into exempt assets in Chapter 2.

When it comes to liens, an asset protection specialist will have many plans for you. He can eliminate those liens that are eligible. Some judgment liens can be eliminated, especially if they're on exempt assets, but those liens that involve alimony or child support payments cannot be eliminated. Other types of liens *can* be made invalid. This approach is particularly useful for consensual and statutory liens. For example, tax and mechanic's liens need to be filed properly and in a timely manner, or they will run the risk of being invalidated. These are issues that your asset protection specialist needs to be aware of.

If it's already time for bankruptcy proceedings, you may be able to get a lien stripped or bifurcated. Essentially, you're stripping the lien of some of its value through a court proceeding. This often happens when the value of a property drops by the time the bankruptcy is filed, even if the lien existed years earlier.

Most of the time, the lien to your personal residence (usually a mortgage) can't be stripped. There are exceptions, however. The first occurs when the lien isn't based solely on the home or personal residence, but on some other property as well. In these cases, lien stripping—reducing the creditor's interest in your property—is allowed. Second, some bankruptcy courts allow second mortgages to be bifurcated in court. Third, lien stripping is allowed in all property that you don't actually reside in.

In short, there are as many ways to combat liens against you as there are liens in the world. As a real estate investor, you need to be on guard against as many as possible, and swat them off like mosquitoes in the heat of summer. With so many dangers lurking, it's no surprise that asset protection is so important for everyone, no matter how much money you have in the bank.

# Overcoming Barriers to Asset Protection— *Do It Right or Don't Do It at All*

CHAPTER

There's one simple reason why you shouldn't try to safeguard your assets by yourself: There's just too much to know. There are people who make a living deciphering the government's laws and rulings about asset protection disputes, the transfer of assets, and filing for bankruptcy. With fifty states in the U.S., each with a differing set of laws, the American debtor faces a minefield of litigation, where everything from internal emails to telephone records can tell creditors how much money you have and where it is. These issues alone make it almost impossible to truly protect your assets without an attorney or a CPA—or preferably both (we use both at Anderson Business Advisors). Here are some examples of why people need professional help.

> Tim sells his house and transfers the proceeds from the sale into a Nevada limited liability company. Six months later, Tim is accused of trying to hide assets from his creditors through that transfer. Tim is confused—how could a transfer that occurred before the lawsuit be under suspicion? He hopes it's a mistake, but his new attorney is telling him otherwise.

> Annie has a small lakefront cabin in Maine that she decides to give to her grandson for a graduation present. If she had kept it, she might lose it to the IRS for the back income taxes she owes, and Annie's accountant prefers that she remain insolvent (no assets). But her attorney warns her that she might be accused of defrauding the IRS. The IRS isn't impressed with the maneuvering. Annie is confused—how can a gift be fraudulent?

Tim and Annie thought they were savvy investors, but, in reality, they weren't aware of some of the obstacles to asset protection. There are many federal and state laws that apply to the transfer of assets—whether those assets are cash, stock, real estate, or luxury goods. Made at the right time and for the right reasons, asset transfers are the main mechanism of a good asset protection plan. Made at the wrong time and for the wrong reasons, asset transfers can do more than just leave your assets vulnerable to creditors: They could be deemed fraudulent transfers and lead to fines and penalties, and possible litigation by federal and state governments—even if you didn't plan on committing a crime, or even if you did not know the law existed! Trust me, transferring your assets blindly, without a long-term plan to avoid litigation and taxation, is almost always a dangerous maneuver.

There are many issues involved in asset transfers. Most of the time, asset protection involves moving assets from non-exempt status (such as cash) to exempt status (such as those things outlined in Chapter 3) in an effort to avoid future or present creditors from attaching them in a lawsuit. The timing, amounts, and types of these transfers are critical, and a false move could result in huge financial and emotional losses, not to mention jail time. With so much at stake, it's simply foolish not to take advantage of the opportunities to safeguard your hard-earned money—and your peace of mind—by doing it with professional help.

This chapter will outline two areas where transfers may be considered fraudulent (made with intent to defraud) and what kind of weapons creditors have to attach the assets you're trying to transfer or already have transferred.

## THE UNIFORM FRAUDULENT TRANSFERS ACT (UFTA)

Even the most honest investor can run afoul of The Uniform Fraudulent Transfers Act (UFTA). This is the primary regulation that gives creditors power over you. Though it's a federal act, some states have their own versions—which adopt virtually all the provisions of the federal UFTA. The UFTA not only provides creditors with ways to reach the assets of their debtors, it also defines the terms *creditors* and *debtors*.

Well, sort of.

A creditor is someone with a claim to a payment. A debtor is someone with a claim of payment against him (a liability), even if the new claim against you has no merit. An asset is any property that isn't exempt (like those that are listed in the next chapter) and doesn't have a valid lien on it. Sound vague? That's the point. The UFTA likes to keep things open to broad interpretations, which unfortunately increases threats against your assets.

The UFTA's primary purpose is defining when and what asset transfers are fraudulent. This allows creditors to get at assets that you thought were safely out of reach. The UFTA was enacted to catch those people who try to appear broke, or insolvent, in order to avoid their creditors. That's fraud. However, because the UFTA's definitions are so broad, it may seem almost impossible to predict what type of transfer is considered fraudulent and what isn't.

For starters, the UFTA outlines two types of fraud:

1. **Actual Fraud:** This is a no-brainer. You made the transfer with the intent of avoiding a debt. Your intent is proven with evidence from the court. This is the biggest threat your asset transfers face, and it's discussed in detail below.
2. **Constructive Fraud:** This takes a little explaining. Constructive fraud is when the creditor thinks you're being sneaky by "giving away" your assets when you're insolvent. It essentially comes up when the court decides that an asset you gave away as a gift was actually a fraudulent transfer. The most obvious indication is that you were insolvent when the transfer was made. In this case, your intent is irrelevant. That's right, even if you didn't intend to cheat anyone, the court can decide, based on the creditor's case, that you did cheat someone.

So how does the UFTA decide what's actual fraud and what's constructive fraud? There are four basic factors in evaluating potentially fraudulent transfers (and some of these may look familiar from our examples).

### ISSUES IN DETERMINING FRAUDULENT TRANSFERS:

**TIMING**: Was the claim brought during the four-year statute of limitations?
**SOLVENCY**: Did the debtor have more assets or more liabilities during the the time of the transfer?
**VALUE**: Did the debtor receive a "reasonably equivalent value" for the asset?
**INTENT**: What does all the evidence show about the debtor's intent?

With these questions in mind, let's look at how the court evaluates cases of actual and constructive fraud.

Remember Tim and his Nevada limited liability company? He thought he was being clever in avoiding any complications by transferring the money. Now he faces creditors who want to get at that money, all asking the questions I listed on the previous page.

The first question is timing—*delay in creating your plan may cause undue suffering.* A statute of limitations states the maximum number of years between the transfer and the creditor's claim being brought in court. In Tim's case, his creditor brought the claim within the four-year statute of limitations. Though it varies in some states, four years is generally the statute of limitation for fraudulent transfer claims. Sometimes, the lawyers get clever and argue that the statute of limitations period starts running one year from when the transfer should have been discovered—even if it's been more than four years. In short—almost anything is possible.

The second issue is solvency—which is a fancy way of asking if you're broke. If you're solvent, then your assets are greater than your liabilities, and you are able to pay your debts. If you're insolvent, then your liabilities are greater than your assets, and you aren't able to pay your debts. If you make transfers when you're insolvent, courts will wonder why you're transferring money away at a time when you need it the most. The simplest way that most courts determine solvency is the "balance sheet" test—simply add up the assets and liabilities. However, the list of liabilities usually includes *the current claim(s) against you, even if they are incredibly weak.* If your liabilities are greater than your assets—including these new, unproven claims—then you're considered insolvent, and it's probable that your transfer will be counted as fraudulent, regardless of your actual intent in making the transfer. In Tim's case, it turns out that he still has more assets than liabilities, so he's not insolvent by UFTA standards.

The next issue is value. Did you get your money's worth on the transfer? In most cases, the court asks that the transfer resulted in *reasonably equivalent value* for the debtor. This usually translates into fair market value, but not always. In fact, some courts think it's fine if you get half the fair market value as a result of the transfer. In Tim's case, he lost only the banking fees, so the court decides that he got the reasonably equivalent value for his transfer.

Finally, there's the issue of intent. This is perhaps the most important part of the UFTA, since your intent is not established just by saying what it was. The courts, the lawyers, and your creditors can look at all sorts of evidence to prove your intent—even interrogating witnesses when necessary. Tim is going to have to answer a lot of questions about why he transferred so much money to offshore accounts, including:

- Why did you make the transfer?
- Why didn't you tell your creditors about the transfer?
- Were you being sued by anyone when you made the transfer?
- How much debt were you in?
- Were you anticipating bankruptcy?
- How many of your assets were transferred?
- Did you try to hide assets or escape your debts?
- Was a family member involved?
- Did you have a plan to pay off your debts when they were incurred?

After some grueling sessions, the court decides that Tim never intended to defraud his creditors. The transfer included only a quarter of his assets, and he wasn't being sued by anyone. He had reasonable debt, but wasn't insolvent, and had no reason to report the transfer. He wasn't getting into a debt he couldn't handle, and he was anticipating some money in the future to take care of the debts he had. In short—he had played fair, and so the court decides that his transfer was not fraudulent, and therefore the limited liability company assets are out of reach from the creditors' claims. Phew!

Remember Annie and her lakefront cabin? She wasn't so lucky. Annie was accused of constructive fraud, which is rarer but no less a threat to your assets. In constructive fraud, your intent doesn't matter. In Annie's case, the court simply looked at the first three issues: timing, solvency, and value.

Assuming that the creditor brought the claim in time, the issue of solvency also doesn't bring good news for Annie. She was insolvent at the time of the transfer—even without this new liability against her. A good asset protection specialist would never have allowed her to make that gift to her grandson when she was insolvent, since that almost automatically makes the transfer fraudulent.

To make matters worse, Annie flunks the last test, too. Giving the lakefront cabin away as a gift to her grandson means that she didn't receive "reasonably equivalent value" for her property. She didn't receive anything at all! It's this sort of thing that immediately smells fishy to creditors—and the courts.

Annie never intended to defraud anyone. She wasn't even thinking about her taxes, just her grandson and his graduation—but poor Annie won't get to argue the issue of intent. In cases of constructive fraud, intent doesn't matter; the court doesn't even address it. Annie's lakefront cabin is deemed a fraudulent transfer, and it is added to the list of assets that her creditors—including the IRS—can get to in litigation. So much for being a savvy investor.

Tim and Annie thought that timing was the only factor involved in deciding when a transfer could be determined as fraudulent, but they were wrong. The UFTA is not easy to understand, and without the right experts to guide you, it's very possible to find your transfers questioned and scrutinized—and your assets not nearly as protected as you once thought they were. The UFTA gives creditors broad-ranging powers to attach your assets to their claim, getting at the savings you thought were safe and clear.

But the UFTA is not the only barrier to asset protection. There's also every investor's nightmare: bankruptcy.

## BANKRUPTCY

Filing for bankruptcy isn't quite as simple as it may sound. I've had numerous clients who thought that filing for bankruptcy is simply admitting you're broke and having all the debts against you wiped out. Unfortunately, it's not usually as clear-cut as that.

First of all, you have to choose one of the three ways of filing for bankruptcy—Chapter 7 (the most common way), Chapter 13 (for people, not companies), and Chapter 11 (for companies, not people). Then you have to figure out which of your assets can be attached by the court to pay your creditors. That's right—bankruptcy doesn't make all your creditors magically disappear, and it only works on certain types of creditors, for certain debts. The court liquidates all your non-exempt assets to pay the creditors first in line (usually secured creditors, or the government). When all that money runs out, the leftover creditors and their debts are "discharged". It's these debts that are wiped out, but there's a strong likelihood that you won't now be "debt-free." In fact, many of the bigger debts that you're trying to run away from may not be eliminated at all! Bankruptcy gives the creditors some of your money, leaves you some of your money, and may leave some of your debts for you to pay back later. This is all litigated in bankruptcy courts in front of bankruptcy judges. And the rules of asset transfers both before and after filing for bankruptcy are complicated.

Let's get back to the issue of exempt assets as opposed to non-exempt assets, and which asset transfers are allowed by the court and which are considered fraudulent. Here are some examples.

James, a former marketing executive, retires and decides to file for bankruptcy. A golfing buddy tells him that Florida has an almost unlimited homestead exemption—meaning that if James moves to Florida, his house will be exempt from any bankruptcy proceedings. James goes with his gut. He moves to Florida, buys a $1,000,000 house, and five months later files for bankruptcy.

Kelly and Jake decide to invest $500,000 in an offshore trust, which Jake heard about in a late-night television seminar. Kelly wants to use the money to buy life insurance policies or to fund an IRA, but Jake has a plan: They'll file for bankruptcy and live on the money from the offshore trust. After all, since the money isn't located in the United States, he won't have to report it, right?

Her funds running low, Sophia defaults on her student loans and on her installment plan to pay back taxes. She decides to file for bankruptcy to get rid of the whole mess. Sophia decides to enter into a partnership with her friend Carter and to buy a glass-bottom boat to take tourists around the local colorful reefs. She figures the business will help her keep afloat after the bankruptcy proceedings take care of her debts.

Sometimes a little knowledge is a dangerous thing. James and Jake are getting their information from sources that don't know all the ins and outs of bankruptcy. They're making transfers that could be deemed fraudulent in almost any state jurisdiction, not to mention running afoul of the UFTA. Both James' Florida house and Kelly and Jake's offshore trust are going to be included in their bankruptcy litigation. Sophia is in even worse trouble. Bankruptcy solves none of her problems, and that glass-bottom boat might even add to them!

Instead of taking the advice of well-meaning friends, golfing buddies, and impersonal television pitchmen, these people should have been calling up an asset protection specialist to guide them through their options. As it stands, their asset transfers leave them wide open to the creditors who might have dealt more leniently with them if they hadn't filed for bankruptcy. Let's take each example one by one.

James is right. Florida does have a very broad homestead exception (meaning that the entire $1,000,000 would be exempt under Florida's bankruptcy law), but the timing of his transfer was fatally flawed. By waiting only five months to declare bankruptcy after buying his $1 million Florida house and then trying to take advantage of the homestead exception, James made a fraudulent transfer. Florida's homestead exception in bankruptcy has a residency requirement of forty months—meaning that James would have had to live in Florida for at least forty months before filing for bankruptcy to take advantage of the law regarding home exemption. Because of the poor timing of his asset transfer, James' $1,000,000 purchase must be listed when he filed for bankruptcy and is an attachable asset. His attempt to move from non-exempt asset (cash) to exempt asset (Florida house) failed.

Kelly and Jake fell for the wrong information in a flashy late-night infomercial that promoted offshore trusts as the most effective form of asset protection. Just because it's not in the United States doesn't mean you don't have to report it in the bankruptcy proceeding! When Jake and Kelly file, they'll be forced to report their $500,000 to their creditors, and they'll realize the hard way that the offshore trust account was about as safe as hiding bundles of cash under their mattress. However, if they had followed Kelly's advice and put it into an ERISA-approved retirement plan at the right time then they might have saved the entire $500,000!

As for Sophia, bankruptcy is simply not an option. There are certain types of debts and creditors that bankruptcy cannot discharge. If all the assets are liquidated, and these specific non-dischargable debts are not paid during the bankruptcy proceedings, you still have to pay them yourself in the future. For the most part, these non-dischargeable debts include:

- Student loans
- Federal, state, and local taxes
- Debts arising from fraud, embezzlement, or other violations of the law
- Alimony, maintenance, and child support payments
- Any fines or penalties arising when intoxicated
- Debts incurred by purchase of luxury goods worth more than $1,000 within 60 days of filing of the bankruptcy
- Any debts not listed on the bankruptcy petition

Sophia's student loans and back taxes aren't available for discharge, no matter how the bankruptcy plays out. Moreover, that glass-bottomed boat might even be considered a luxury good worth more than $1,000. Sophia could argue that the boat is part of her business and therefore exempt, but she's hit another snag: exemptions are available for natural people (sole proprietorships) but not for corporate entities such as LLCs, corporations, and partnerships! Since she's in a limited partnership with Carter, Sophia gets no exemptions. Even worse, the boat is not protected and must be tallied in as an asset in the bankruptcy proceedings. Sophia has just made things worse for herself (and for Carter!).

Filing for bankruptcy can be ugly, with both sides facing potential heavy losses. In Sophia's case, her creditors might have been more willing to deal with her before being pulled into bankruptcy court! Additionally, filing for bankruptcy carries with it some hefty baggage. It remains on your credit report for 10 years, and will affect every purchase you make. However, if you engage in fraudulent transfers to move your money around before a bankruptcy, then your credit report may be the least of your problems. Those transfers could leave you wide open to creditors ready to gut your bank account to get their money back and worse, leave you open to criminal penalties.

There are criminal penalties against those who:

- Knowingly and fraudulently conceal any property
- Knowingly and fraudulently receive property after the beginning of the bankruptcy action in order to "outwit" the Bankruptcy Code
- Knowingly and fraudulently conceal or transfer any property with the intent of the defeating the Code, while serving as an officer for an entity or business contemplating bankruptcy

Bankruptcy is not a get-rich-quick scheme or a fast way to get out of debt. In some ways, you were jumping out of the frying pan and right into the fire. If done properly, bankruptcy can be a useful tool to deal with debt—as long as there's some ethical pre-bankruptcy planning.

To make matters even more daunting, there's a lot of bankruptcy reform legislation pending. In the years after the Internet bubble burst, Chapter 7 filings exploded, and creditor lobbies pushed to restrict asset transfers even more. The reformers are working on restrictions on exemptions and time limits for transfers, as well as limited access to the variety of bankruptcy filings available. Chapter 7 filing is the most common form of bankruptcy, but it doesn't protect against all debts. Any property that has a valid consensual or statutory lien on it (mortgage or state taxes, for example) must still be paid off. After bankruptcy, the bank still owns your house, and you have to keep making payments. In practice, most bankruptcy debtors retain a portion of their assets, but as bankruptcy reforms are pushed forward, that may change.

As for the other types of bankruptcy, they have their own limitations. In Chapter 13 the debtor sets up a three-year plan to pay off all the creditors. This is usually to avoid a wholesale liquidation of assets or surrendering of property to the creditors, and the debtor can arrange his own repayment plan. However, the debtor has to account for all his assets, liabilities, and transfers during that three-year period. To make matters worse for the debtor, bankruptcy reformers want to extend that period to five years.

Chapter 11 is for commercial or corporate entities, and that bankruptcy filing is known as restructuring. This is the primary way that large organizations manage to stay in business after filing for bankruptcy; the restructuring of the company continues the operations.

As you can see, bankruptcy (and the issue of asset transfers) is vitally important to a good asset protection plan. Along with avoiding litigation and tax liability, asset protection should involve some pre-bankruptcy planning as well. You may think it's easy to transfer money (assets), but your creditors have many weapons in their arsenal to get to your assets. Your weapons? Your exemptions.

# Exempt Assets— *No Sense in Protecting What Is Already Protected*

CHAPTER

I've used the term "exempt" numerous times, and now it's time to take a good, hard look at what qualifies as exempt assets. These are assets you already own that are exempt from creditors—already protected by statute or regulations, either at the state or federal level. Not knowing what assets are considered exempt—or, in some cases, what percentage of the value of the asset is exempt—is just plain dumb. Not only are you essentially asking to pay more than your share, but you're also missing golden opportunities to protect your hard-earned savings from creditors, excessive taxation, or greedy litigants. Asset protection specialists know the ins and outs of asset exemptions like the backs of their hands.

Each state has differing regulations regarding asset exemptions. Think of them as "loopholes" in the many laws that protect creditors in bankruptcy courts and in litigation. Some states are generous with exemptions: Florida and Texas, for example, offer more than 35 separate exemptions—above and beyond federal and bankruptcy court exemptions. Other states offer fewer loopholes to safeguard your money. In this chapter, I'll discuss the more popular exemptions—the ones most likely to save you the most money.

**Exemptions**
a) Homestead
b) IRA and pension plans
c) Annuities
d) Life Insurance
e) Social Security

Though these exemptions are the ones most likely to save you the big bucks, there are many more out there. Depending on what state you live in, your Bible, your commercial-grade lawnmower, your big-screen television, and your liquor license may all be assets that are exempt from liens and bankruptcies. Professional planners know how to maximize your exemptions and can advise you on how to spend, transfer, and invest your money so that it is litigation-proof and creditor-proof.

## HOMESTEAD

The homestead exemption, which applies to your place of residence, is one of the most important exemptions you can claim. The homestead exemption is usually stated as a percentage or dollar amount of the value of your personal residence that is exempt from creditors. The amount varies widely from state to state. In addition to Florida and Texas, the states Kansas, Iowa, and South Dakota provide debtor friendly homestead exemptions, allowing you to write off an unlimited dollar amount related to the value of your home. Other states, such as Delaware, the District of Columbia, New Jersey, and Pennsylvania, offer no specific homestead exemption. All other states fall somewhere in between unlimited exemption and no exemption. Under federal law, the bankruptcy homestead exemption is $20,200 which, depending on where you live, could be a lot or very little of the value of your home.

But homestead exemptions have their limits.

> Trent moves to Miami and buys an acre of land within city limits. When he goes bankrupt building his dream house on the plot, he's shocked to realize that the Florida homestead exemption applies only to a half-acre within the city, and that his new family home may not be an exempt asset. Panicking, he calls up Tim, a professional asset planner. He gets some good news: In many cases, this rule is not very strictly enforced. If worse comes to worst, a good portion of Trent's homestead will still be exempt from lawsuits or excessive taxation.

Still, it's best to remember that homestead exemptions can't be applied to all types of liens. Your mortgage, for example, isn't going to go away because of a homestead exception or bankruptcy, even if the entire house is exempt.

So, without a state-by-state evaluation, let's look at some general guidelines for choosing a homestead exemption. (See Appendix A) Consider the following example:

> Carson, a college professor, buys a farmhouse in Iowa for $200,000, with a mortgage of $100,000. A few years later, he gets some book royalties worth $100,000. His investment advisor suggests he pay off the mortgage. Why? By doing so, he gets to turn his non-exempt asset (cash in the bank) into an exempt asset (the farmhouse, under Iowa's unlimited homestead exemption). Carson shrugs off the advice and retires early, planning to live off the money. A few years later, an environmental flaw is found on the land, and Carson is slammed with $100,000 in fees. If Carson had followed his planner's good advice, that original $100,000 in book royalties might have been converted to an exempt asset—the

farmhouse—rather than being vulnerable to government liens.

This brings us to the first rule of homestead exemption:

 **Golden Rule of Homestead Exemption**

*When the state homestead exemption is more than the house value, start paying off mortgages and make your home debt-free.*

Essentially, your entire house is protected under these circumstances—so why wouldn't you want to take advantage of it and keep your money in your pockets where it belongs? Plus, the house is now an unencumbered asset, both free of mortgages and protected from judicial liens.

Here's another example:

> Marcy is a radio DJ living in a $40,000 condo in Cleveland, Ohio. The house has a $20,000 mortgage on it, and Marcy's friend, an asset protection specialist, advises her to get another $15,000 mortgage. Marcy takes her friend's advice and gets the $15,000 in mortgages. Unfortunately, she gets sued for something she says on the air, and she has to file for bankruptcy to satisfy the settlement. Luckily for Marcy, her house is an exempt asset.

If Marcy had ignored her friend's advice, she would have ignored the second rule of Homestead exemptions:

## 2ND Golden Rule of Homestead Exemption

*When the state homestead exemption is less than the house value, put extra consensual liens (such as mortgages) on the property.*

How much debt should you put on your home? Here's a simple equation: The amount of the (property value) minus (homestead exemption) minus (consensual liens) = the amount of your homestead that's vulnerable to liens.

In Marcy's case, that's: ($40,000) minus ($5,000—Ohio's exemption) minus ($20,000 mortgage) = $15,000. This is the amount that is now covered with her new mortgage for $15,000, and that is now protected in bankruptcy court. Thanks to the advice of Marcy's investment planning friend, that is!

There's one special-case rule of homestead exemptions:

## 3RD Golden Rule of Homestead Exemption

*When the state homestead exemption is zero, or very low relative to the house value, consider putting the house in tenancy by the entirety.*

**Warning:** This strategy requires a deep and abiding trust in your spouse. In the states that offer this option, a homestead held by the tenancy of the entirety is often times completely out of the reach of creditors. This is because these states recognize the married couple as a single unit, and one spouse can't transfer property without the consent of the other. But there are limits. If the married couple is in business together, the exemption doesn't protect against debts that the couple accrued together and for which they are jointly liable.

Not all states that have high homestead exemptions recognize this type of ownership either.

Finally, no matter where you live, there are the fourth and fifth rules of homestead exemptions:

 **Golden Rule of Homestead Exemption**

*Always record your exemptions at the county recording office!*

Even though only seventeen states require the recording of a homestead exemption, it's better to be safe than sorry. And finally:

 **Golden Rule of Homestead Exemption**

*Never contribute the home to a business entity such as an LLC, corporation, or partnership.*

Remember that exemptions apply to natural persons, not business entities. However, trusts are often exempt if you properly reserve your exemption.

Homestead exemptions can minimize your liability exposure to litigation, so talk to your asset protection specialist about how to make the most of your exemptions by applying the Golden Rules of Homestead Exemption to your situation.

## IRAS AND PENSION PLANS

There are many varieties of retirement plans that are exempt from creditors and would-be plaintiffs. Whether it's a 401(k), 403(b), 457, or 401(a), these employer-sponsored plans help you in a variety of ways. Once the territory of large corporations, these plans are increasingly utilized by small businesses to benefit the business owners. Plans such as defined contribution plans 401(a) allow a business owner to contribute up to $44,000 per year to his retirement plan. And something many people do not know is that the contribution comes from the business and not the business owner, thereby allowing the business to deduct the entire contribution. Other types of plans are similar in nature but offer even greater contributions.

> John has a small consulting corporation named Amis, Inc. that generates $350,000 in annual profit. After paying himself $200,000 in salary, John seeks advice from his CPA on how he can reduce the remaining $150,000 in income taxable to Amis, Inc. After a meeting with his CPA that was short on time and ideas, John approaches an asset protection specialist about his dilemma. John is surprised to learn about a defined benefit plan that will allow his corporation to contribute $95,000 a year into a retirement account for John. The best part is that it's tax deductible to Amis, Inc. For John's business, this amounted to more than $30,000 in annual tax savings and, like other ERISA-qualified plans, the plan assets are exempt from John's creditors.

What makes these plans so valuable? ERISA. Now who or what is ERISA? The federal Employee Retirement Income Security Act, or ERISA, is the standard by which tax-qualified retirement plans are created. ERISA-qualified plans have been ruled exempt in courts of law, and are excluded from bankruptcy proceedings. A plan that does not meet ERISA standards is pretty poor protection for your money, because without ERISA qualification, you can't be sure your retirement assets are protected. In this way, ERISA gives federal law more power than state law over our retirement plans, giving them exempt status.

Remember John? Now we fast-forward 10 years to find him embroiled in a lawsuit over the extent of damages suffered by one of his Amis, Inc. clients. The disgruntled client successfully sued John individually and also Amis, Inc. for $1,000,000. John's major assets consist of his residence in Florida with $1,200,000 in equity and his $4,000,000 in retirement assets. Fortunately for John, both assets are beyond the reach of his creditor. His Florida house has an unlimited homestead exemption, and his retirement assets are protected under ERISA. Even better for John, his attorney tells him that any proceeds he receives from his retirement plan will be protected. John's attorney tells him to retire.

There are three elements of an ERISA-qualified savings plan: The first is that the plan contains a clause that specifically forbids you from transferring your interest in the plan to someone else. This is called an anti-alienation clause. There are some federal exceptions to the anti-alienation clause, which allow retirement assets to be "assigned" or transferred, to a spouse, child, or other dependent. The second element is that the plan is tax-qualified under Section 401 of the Internal Revenue Code. Who makes the decision about tax-qualification? Unfortunately, that distinction is made within the Government's sole discretion. Finally, there must be one employee covered who is not the employer's spouse or the employer himself/herself.

With all the hoopla about ERISA, you might be surprised to know that there are many plans not covered by this powerful federal regulation. IRAs, for example, are not covered by ERISA, but are covered by state law—which naturally varies from state to state. In some cases, states have decided that only part of the IRA is exempt. In others, all of the IRA is exempt. There are other factors—some states exclude more recent contributions or assets that have been rolled over (transferred) from other accounts. For the most part, states try to decide what part of the retirement funds are "reasonably necessary" to support you and your dependents. Lots of lawsuits take place to decide what, exactly, is included in the definition of "legally necessary".

Whatever form your retirement account takes, you need to know what the state and federal laws are, and how ERISA applies to you. Otherwise, your retirement savings might not go toward your golden years, but into the pockets of lawyers and government agencies.

## ANNUITIES

An annuity is a periodic, fixed payment from a set fund or trust. There are two broad types of annuities: commercial and private.

> Connie takes out a life insurance policy that will pay her an annuity, or monthly payment, in her golden years. She knows that commercial annuities like this one exempt assets. Initially, she transferred her cash (non-exempt) into the larger fund (exempt). Now she's getting exempt cash payments each month, and most of her money is protected in the annuity, which will be exempt from creditors.

Connie has purchased a commercial annuity. In addition to life insurance, there are many other types of annuities, including certain types of pension plans that pay retirement benefits in annuities. The states protect annuities in varying ways, with Texas and Florida once again leading the way in exempting the entire value of the annuities. In other states, the exempt amount is limited by dollar value or by what is only "reasonably necessary" to support the debtor and her dependents. That amount can vary greatly by state. (Big surprise!)

Though the annuities exemption is made to primarily protect commercial annuities, private annuities are also protected.

> Crag is ready to retire after making a killing in the stock market and wants to go to Nantucket to start a charter plane service. He transfers half his net worth —$2,000,000—into an annuity for his life and thereafter to his children. The annuity will in turn pay him $5,000 a month for his living expenses. Crag mistakenly believes he has protected his money, and also significantly reduced any gift taxes that would have arisen if he had just transferred the money to his children's accounts. But, without knowing how Massachusetts deals with annuity exemptions—and how they are limited—Crag's money may not be as safe as he thinks it is.

> Tracy has a different plan to cash in on the annuities exemption—with a private annuity. She owns a valuable painting that is worth $100,000. She sells it to her lawyer grandson Carter—on an installment plan, of course. In exchange for the painting, Carter must pay his grandma Tracy a fixed, periodic, equal payment with a minimum interest rate set by the IRS. This interest rate will be less than commercial interest rates and the expected appreciation of the asset sold. This way, Tracy can give Carter the painting, but still have enough to live on. A private annuity is similar to an installment sale. However, unlike an installment sale, in a private annuity transaction the purchaser only pays until the seller dies. So if Carter paid Tracy $20,000 toward the purchase price of the

painting, upon Tracy's death the remaining $80,000 is tax free to Carter.

Because of the many exemptions surrounding them, many states make it difficult for creditors to get to your annuities. However, the structuring of annuities can be very complex and sophisticated in order for the purchaser to be completely protected. Many people opt for a simpler alternative: the life insurance plan.

## LIFE INSURANCE

Money from life insurance is considered an exempt asset, but, as usual, each state has a different rule for how much of the proceeds are exempt, and for how long. In fact, there are different rules in different states for the owners, the insured, and the beneficiary of the life insurance! Generally speaking, the exemption protects the cash value of the life insurance and, in most cases, the death benefit. It all depends, but there's the usual worry: If you move your money from a non-exempt status (cash) to an exempt status (life insurance), you may be accused of a fraudulent transfer when you pay those premiums. However, in most cases, your creditors will find it hard to prove your intent to defraud in life insurance cases. Why? Because life insurance is a gray area. We don't buy it for investment value; we buy it to take care of our loved ones in an emergency. The cash value of the insurance policy may be exempt, but that doesn't encompass the real value of life insurance. States do recognize the value of protecting the debtor's family—his spouse and dependents—rather than having everyone

*For a detailed state specific list of exemptions go to www.andersonadvisors.com, register for a Platinum membership, then search our interactive map of state specific asset protection topics.*

end up on the street after a bankruptcy case. But before you rush out and buy life insurance, know the limits of the exemptions.

> Roger's grandmother dies, leaving Roger the sole beneficiary of her $1,000,000 life insurance proceeds. Roger wants to invest wisely and takes an asset protection class. There's a lot of information, and someone tells Roger that his insurance proceeds aren't exempt since they are converted from exempt asset (life insurance) to non-exempt asset (cash). Roger, justifiably nervous, decides to hire a specialist in asset planning instead of doing it himself. He learns that his assets experienced an **involuntary conversion** when they moved from Grandma's life insurance plan to cash proceeds. However, life insurance proceeds are a special case, and Roger's $1,000,000 is going to be exempt for many years. Still, Roger keeps records and follows his investment planner's advice.
>
> After their children move out of their house, Bob and his wife Cindy decide to sell their $400,000 house in Chicago, Illinois, and sail around the world for fourteen months. But Bob, a past portfolio investment manager, knows that selling this house means converting his homestead (an exempt asset) into cash (a non-exempt asset). Unlike life insurance, the proceeds from a homestead conversion are only protected for one year in Illinois, so Bob knows they can't count on the whole $400,000 being protected after he and his wife return from their trip. With help, he plans accordingly.

In Bob's case, he learns that homestead conversions, unlike life insurance payments, do have their time limits. In many cases, like Roger's, life insurance policies aren't owned by individuals, but by trusts. As long as everyone is honest and the monies funded into the trust pay the life insurance premiums, the trust and the assets should be out of reach from creditors at a bankruptcy hearing or in a lawsuit.

If you don't already know it, creditors, whether credit card companies, an overly litigious tenant, or the government, have whole systems of laws in their favor. With broad rules from the UFTA (explained in Chapter 1) and the movement toward bankruptcy reform, your money is far more vulnerable than it ever was before. If you know the full power of your exemptions, and how the right transfer at the right time can save you money, then you have a fighting chance in our lawsuit-happy society. You have to think very defensively about your money in order to protect it. And sometimes that can mean hiding it.

If there's one over-arching theme to my work at Anderson Business Advisors, it's this: Don't look rich. The more money you have, the less protected you are against threats of litigation. Why? It's simple—people don't sue poor people. There's no point. But if you're sitting on a fat bank account, be ready for some unsavory types poking around your savings.

On the other hand, if your money is hidden safely off the charts—in a manner that's totally legal and on the up-and-up—then you're less likely to be hassled by creditors. They can't get at funds they don't know about, or that are exempt assets.

How poor should you look? As poor as possible. In fact, as I like to joke with my clients, you should look as if you qualify for food stamps. And that's the subject of the next chapter. You can find additional information on the varying state laws regarding exempt assets at www.andersonadvisors.com. Sign up there as a member, and then search any state you like for a detailed list of assets and their exemptions.

# Anonymity in Asset Protection Planning— *Appear To Qualify for Food Stamps*

CHAPTER

At this point, you may be wondering if I'm serious about the food stamps. I'm not, but that should be the way you think: "I own nothing." Anyone can get a list of your assets to see how much you're worth, whom you owe, and whether you'd be good to lend to, or to sue. The less that's public record or under your name, the better. I often joke with my students when I teach a class that the best form of asset protection is to own nothing and do nothing . . . in your own name. We will address those points later, but for right now an inexpensive and relatively easy form of asset protection is my food stamp approach.

Attorneys, like everyone else, have expenses and a desire to make a living. If an attorney's income is based on what he collects for his client in a lawsuit, then a successful attorney will make darn sure the person he is suing has assets. Your plan should be to make the plaintiff's attorney's job extremely difficult by making yourself appear worthless when viewed from afar. The attorney must then decide, do I take the case and put in considerable time, effort, and expense, or do I look for easier prey? The answer seems fairly obvious—there are plenty of people who are fully exposed and will make for much easier pickings.

Here's an example of a food stamp approach:

Carly rents her apartment from Leif, who owns three buildings in the area. One day she slips and falls in the apartment. She claims that she slipped because the air conditioner had been leaking water into the floor, but Leif knows he checked the air conditioner just last week. Unfortunately, he didn't keep any records. Carly goes to her lawyer and wants to file a suit against Leif for negligence, with a claim of damages of $100,000. Her lawyer investigates Leif's net assets, and realizes that Leif doesn't have anywhere near that kind of money. All three of his properties are heavily mortgaged, so Leif really isn't worth suing. Sensing that this case would not be worth his time, the lawyer persuades Carly not to sue.

And it's as simple as that. If a would-be creditor or future litigant looks into your affairs, he should see that you aren't worth suing. Judgment creditors are especially discouraged when they realize that their potential target has minimal cash in hand, or that all his assets are exempt from creditors. I have seen this strategy used very effectively in lawsuits where plaintiff's counsel is more than willing to dismiss defendants who appear to have no assets. What is unfortunate, but true, is that many times the most culpable party gets dismissed for lack of assets and the party who had little or nothing to do with the claimed damages is stuck fighting the battle because they have assets. The goals of asset protection—to minimize the risk of litigation and to limit your potential loss—both require that you write off or otherwise make unavailable most of your money.

This kind of thinking is not for the faint-hearted, and it is foolish to attempt it alone. You definitely need an objective opinion, preferably from someone both trained and up to date in the latest asset protection techniques. While a financial planner might help you look poor on the books, he may not know how safe or legal his plan is for you. Similarly, getting a lawyer to help you minimize your legal vulnerability is great, except that the techniques that make you look poor can be very different from just setting up an asset protection entity. Also, the lawyer doesn't have a long-term interest in your situation, and may not create a plan that's a right fit for your particular situation. This can be particularly true in terms of real estate investors, who are involved in secured credit lending. That, if you remember from Chapter 1, means that the loans and money involved are usually tied to property, most likely personal residences, commercial property, and/or rental buildings. This means that the stakes are high, and creditors can and do attach real estate when the payments on the loan (usually a mortgage) are late or insufficient.

You don't actually have to go out and qualify for food stamps, but to minimize the growing threat of litigation, you'd better look like you own nothing. Think about it. The homeless don't get sued. Ever. The purpose behind civil litigation is always to get damages, and a lawyer probably won't take a case where the defendant is worth next to nothing. There's no money in it for him or his client, so he'll start looking for other avenues to resolve the situation. Don't kid yourself that lawyers will take any case on a contingency fee or pro bono (free). They will, but only if they think it's going to pay off big in the end. Don't be that payoff. Keep your assets safe from harm using the latest asset protection planning techniques. For example, a client of mine was recently threatened with a lawsuit. The details are not important, but what the attorney said is all too common. During my first and only conversation with this attorney, I patiently listened as he threatened to bankrupt my clients. After five minutes of his diatribe, I cut him off and told him that I thought his clients were fishing in a dry creek and I wanted to know what this call was really about. The attorney paused, and then said, "It's simple—your clients have a job and money—my clients don't." I told him to go get better clients and hung up.

## EQUITY STRIPPING

Equity stripping is a way of making your real estate assets appear less valuable to lawyers and judgment creditors. When your house has equity, it becomes a target for potential creditors. Additionally, when you get a mortgage to buy a house, the bank and you have totally different views of the value of the house. For you, it's your home and the place where your family lives. If you plan to do some construction or remodeling, or live in nice neighborhood, you might be expecting the value of the house to go up so that when you finally sell it, you make a profit. The bank doesn't view the house as a home or even as a long-term asset. The bank is willing to give you slightly less than what they think the house would get if it were sold at an auction. That's usually the mortgage. The bank thinks short-term; you're thinking long-term. Meanwhile, your creditors have other ideas. Here's an example:

> Corby, a gossip columnist, decides to purchase a $600,000 apartment complex, and gets a $250,000 mortgage on it. When Laverne sues Corby for slander, she wins a $300,000 settlement. Corby sells his apartment for $650,000 to pay her, but he is upset to realize that he has to pay the bank mortgage first. After that, he's left with $400,000, out of which he has to pay Laverne $300,000. Now, with just $100,000 left, Corby has to go back to renting.

Your creditors know that you'll have to pay the bank mortgage—a loan from a secure lender—first, so they'll adjust their plans accordingly. If Corby had gotten a second $350,000 mortgage, Laverne and her lawyer would have seen that the apartment was only worth $50,000 after Corby paid off all the secured creditors. Her lawyer would probably have persuaded Laverne to drop the suit.

That is equity stripping in a nutshell: putting enough debt on a property so that it appears worthless to judgment creditors. After all, why go after someone who has three creditors to pay off before he even gets to you? Better to go after someone whose assets are more available. That's how lawyers, and many creditors, think.

There are a variety of types of equity stripping. The most common is commercial equity stripping. This essentially means that a commercial entity (usually a bank) will lend you money in exchange for an interest in your property. The bank gives you cash and puts a lien on your property. If you transfer the cash to a non-exempt form, you just made a bundle of money and kept your property free of creditors. Commercial equity stripping is a very powerful way to discourage creditors, because they will have to wait in a very long line to get to your assets.

Of course, there are some drawbacks. The bank has all the power in this situation, and you could be foreclosed on if your payments are consistently late or inadequate. You will pay interest to the bank on the money your borrow. And, of course, if the owner is being sued, it's much harder to make regular payments. Banks are also wary of future debt—some will foreclose if a court decides that you're insolvent. Even mortgages, it seems, are not always an easy way to protect your property. Take a look at the following example:

> Frank runs a tailoring service out of his home. He hears about equity stripping from a friend, and decides to go out and get

a second mortgage. Unfortunately, business gets bad and he defaults. The bank forecloses on the house and Frank is in a Catch-22: He can't make payments if he can't work, and he can't work if he doesn't have his house! Because he operated his business out of his residence, commercial equity stripping was actually a very bad idea for him.

Frank made the mistake of assuming that all strategies work for all people. There are many situations where commercial equity stripping works for real estate investors, but I'll just go over a few here to give you an idea.

## HOME EQUITY LINE OF CREDIT

One of the easiest ways to get the full value of your home—and minimize the risk of losing your personal residence—is a home equity line of credit, sometimes known as a HELOC. This is essentially a low-interest, high-credit limit secured loan which allows you to withdraw funds based on the equity value of your home. The nice thing about this option is that you are given a credit card or checkbook which allows you to borrow funds based on the value of your personal residence. This is a secured line of credit that works much like a credit card. The lender agrees to loan you a set sum of money in exchange for a deed of trust against your house. There are numerous advantages to this option as opposed to a second mortgage.

First, unlike a second mortgage, the home equity line of credit does not start accruing interest until you use the line of credit. Second, this method allows you to borrow gradually over time, rather than getting into further debt in one giant lump sum. With its flexibility and the reduced interest rates, a home equity line of credit can save you a lot of money and safeguard your home.

This method allows you to tie up the equity in your property so that would-be creditors can't get to it. This is particularly useful to protect your personal residence. Creditors and lawyers know that the fastest way to get you to pay is to threaten your home, but if you've stripped all the equity from your personal residence, they have less leverage over you.

How does this work? — Here's an example:

> Mike and Lisette own a residence in San Diego, California. In the past two years they have seen the value of their home skyrocket from $800,000 to $1,400,000. Mike and Lisette owe $600,000 and are very concerned about their $800,000 in exposed equity. They speak to their attorney and he tells them to apply for a HELOC to mask their equity. Mike and Lisette obtain a $750,000 line of credit from Bank of America and feel very secure knowing that whoever looks at their home will discover it is encumbered with $1,350,000 of debt leaving only $50,000 of exposed equity. What their attorney did not tell them is that the line of credit acts like a smokescreen but will not protect their equity unless they actually borrow the money.

Mike and Lisette learned the hard way that the advice they received was only half the story when Lisette was sued over a rearend car collision she was involved in on her way home from work. The plaintiff obtained a $700,000 judgment against Lisette and proceeded to attack the equity in her house. The plaintiff's attorney got it.

Mike and Lisette placed the HELOC on their house but did not actually borrow against the equity when they realized they might get sued. As a result, the bank's interest is only secured up to the amount of money actually loaned out to Mike and Lisette. Hence, Mike and Lisette's efforts were defeated because they were not instructed to actually borrow against their equity and to put that money in an exempt entity to protect it. I will show you how to protect your savings in Chapter 9.

I am sure you realize now that an equity line of credit is not the same as a second mortgage. Equity lines of credit do not offer blanket protection and only protect up to the amount of credit actually used by the borrower. So why use it? To make potential creditors think you are worthless, and, hence, not worth the effort and expense of suing.

With a HELOC, you plan to use every last drop of equity in your home, and leave little or nothing for creditors to get at in cases of a judgment against you. You appear poor on the books and have a new line of credit to spend or save as you see fit. But as attractive as the HELOC is for your personal residence, it will not work for your investment property, which also needs to be protected. In those cases, a second mortgage or a secured line of credit may be advisable.

## SECOND MORTGAGES ON RENTAL PROPERTIES

For real estate investors, there is always the option of getting a second mortgage on your property. Remember, the less equity your property has, the less attractive it will be to creditors. But when you're thinking about getting a second mortgage on a rental property, there are some other considerations to think about. Here's an example to get you started:

> Eric has a small brownstone with three units. He loves his tenants, but is thinking about getting a second mortgage on the property to make better use of its equity value. He approaches some residential lenders, but they won't even give him a quote. Eric is confused, until his financial planner

points out that he should be approaching commercial lenders because he doesn't live in the brownstone himself.

Most commercial lenders will require that you still retain at least 20% equity on the property after qualifying for the mortgage. Also, if you don't live in the rental property yourself, you may be required to provide more documentation than you would have if you had actually been living in the property. How much could Eric get? Well, the interest on the second mortgage will be a few percentage points higher than on his first mortgage. The term will be anywhere from 15 to 30 years for repayment. He may be able to get as much as 100% of his brownstone's value, but it is more likely that his commercial lender will cap the amount at 80%, depending on how good Eric's credit is, and on how his documentation reads. The more he gets, the higher his interest rates will be, so it is likely that he won't opt for the whole 100%.

Both an equity line of credit and a second mortgage offer differing protections for your property, but both are clever and legal ways to strip the equity from your property. A potential litigant and his lawyer will think twice about getting in line to receive assets when there are many lenders and other creditors in line ahead of them.

However, why think in terms of a single property? When it comes to these strategies, you can cover multiple properties with one loan. This is referred to as cross-collateralization.

> In addition to his personal residence, Adrian owns two properties: a beach house worth $500,000 and a small cabin in Maine worth $100,000. He wants to do some equity stripping, and so he goes to an asset protection specialist. The asset protection specialist advises Adrian to get a $500,000 loan based on his beach house. But when he gets the agreement,

> Adrian is shocked to learn that he not only has to put up his beach house as collateral, but also his cabin in Maine. The asset protection specialist tells him this is a good thing.

Adrian is getting some good advice. With this cross-collateralization agreement, Adrian is getting a large loan and also stripping his cabin of equity. Technically, the loan is secured by his beach house, but since the loan amount is for the full value of the house, the lender requires additional collateral. However, this works in Adrian's favor because this lender now has a security interest in the cabin as well, stripping it of its equity. If a lawyer does an asset check on Adrian, he'll see that not only is his beach house stripped of equity, but that there's a line of lenders ahead of him for that cabin as well. In most cases, he'll look elsewhere for potential lawsuits.

It is worth mentioning that if you wish to employ this technique you must negotiate with your lender for the "right of substitution". The right of substitution permits you to sell your properties and give the bank additional collateral without having to renegotiate the loan.

## FRIENDLY LIENS AND CONTROLLED EQUITY STRIPPING

As all these examples show, encumbering your properties with liens—also known as debt financing—can be a savvy way to protect your investment and your finances. But commercial lenders can be very difficult to work with or exact harsh terms for the loan. Why go through a bank when you can put liens on your property by yourself, or with the help of trusted family and friends?

In the case of controlled entity stripping, the third party is a friend, family member, a corporation or other entity that you own and control, or any private lender who is willing to be flexible on the terms of the agreement. This is particularly daunting to creditors, since the terms of the loan can make the property unattractive to creditors. However, it's not always a pretty picture. Here's an example:

> Gary enters into a loan agreement with his friend Gregory, and uses his $1,000,000 penthouse apartment as collateral. He gets a line of credit from Gregory for $1,000,000, and Gregory files a lien on the penthouse as collateral. Neither Gregory nor Gary takes the terms of the agreement too seriously because it was done for asset protection purposes and Gary never borrowed the money. However, after Gary's daughter runs off with Gregory's son, the friends begin feuding, and suddenly Gregory starts playing hardball. When Gary wants Gregory to release the lien so Gary can sell his penthouse and move to Hawaii, Gregory refuses. Then the lawyers get involved, and suddenly the penthouse is up for grabs.

Clearly, you have to be careful about who you enter into these loan agreements with. In many cases, it may be wise to turn to the most trustworthy lender you know: you. A friendly lien is simply a lien you put on the property yourself. It looks exactly the same as if you had a third party or commercial lender doing it for you, except, in this case, the third party is a corporate entity you created. A friendly lien is particularly useful for those businesses that have already decided to become a corporate entity and need their assets protected in case of litigation. With a friendly lien, since there's no real third party, there's no danger of your property being repossessed.

Friendly liens are particularly appropriate in some states that have adopted broader asset protection guidelines in an effort to attract small businesses and investors. Delaware has traditionally been the most favorable state for corporate entities, but in recent years Nevada has been aggressively promoting its business benefits. Like Delaware, Nevada charges minimal taxes and fees on entities.

However, some marketers, both online and in-person, claim that Nevada corporate entities are virtually creditor-proof, and that they provide total secrecy in terms of shareholders, boards of directors, and assets. These private corporations—sometimes available online for a few hundred dollars—are generally best used as fire starter for your outdoor fireplace rather than as asset protection. Forming a corporation or any business entity is not as easy as putting up a few hundred dollars for an entity and then thinking you're set. This is a misconception that traps many people in business entities that do little for them in the way of protecting their assets or reducing their taxes. I run into people at every asset protection workshop I teach who were lured into the low-cost approaches to asset protection only to discover they did not buy a car. Instead, they bought four tires and now they want to drive. If you want to create a corporation that protects your identity and your assets, you must work with a professional who understands the law and its nuances. Any entity you create requires much more than filing a piece of paper with a state and paying a fee. You need operating agreements that back up your business and what you're trying to accomplish. Think of it this way: If you want to put together an asset protection plan on the cheap, then just stop there and don't waste your money. Asset protection is not like buying a DVD player, where the $40 player will perform just as well as the $400 player. I often

*Anonymity is crucial when creating your personal equity stripping strategy. Be sure your entity is created in a state that protects the identity of its officers and directors.*

*Anonymity in Asset Protection Planning* 55

ask people: "Would you fly on a plane built by Freddie's Build 'Em Fast and Cheap Airplanes?" Don't bother answering, we both know your response.

As you can guess, privacy is pretty important when it comes to friendly liens. If all the laws are followed properly, then you're doing nothing wrong, but you still don't want it to become public knowledge that the third-party lender is yourself. Otherwise, there's no point in the maneuver, since the goal after all was to hide your assets from financial predators. A third-party lender allows you to encumber your property, strip its equity, and make it poor pickings for creditors and attorneys. Anyone who wants to go after the property in a lawsuit or judgment will have to wait in line for that lender. However, if your creditors know that the third party is just you, then they will work harder to dismantle your asset protection plan to get at your savings. Remember, the whole purpose is to appear poor, and one of the most important aspects of this is to keep your name off the books and out of sight. That, by the way, is why Nevada corporations may still offer more to the real estate investor than the Delaware corporation, since Delaware is the homeland of the "public" company. When it comes to asset protection, "public" is the exact opposite of what you want.

In Nevada you can create a corporation that does not have your name listed as an officer or director. You use someone else as a nominee director and officer for filing purposes and then have that

*To obtain more information on the different business forms go to www.andersonadvisors.com, register for a free Gold membership if you are a first time user, then search our Video section for "Truth About Nevada Corporations" to view a video about incorporating in Nevada.*

person resign. I have created thousands of Nevada entities that protect my clients' identities from attorneys and snoops who are looking for a quick buck, by using this favorable law. If you are seriously considering the friendly lien strategy, then Nevada is a must, and your nominee should be an attorney for added protection. We will get into this in more detail in the following chapters. But understand this—when it comes to creating an asset protection plan, privacy is one of our major asset protection strategies. *If they don't know you own it, then they won't try to take it.*

That said, you shouldn't be solely focused on privacy. This is the mistake that many investors make. Anonymity is very important with regard to friendly liens, but your assets should be protected even if your privacy is blown, because privacy is your first line of defense (i.e. a smokescreen). Here's an example of how this works:

A client of mine in California, who we will refer to as "Dr. Lord", owns four apartment buildings with a total of $1,500,000 in equity among them. Dr. Lord went to the bank to get a line of credit, but the bank refused Dr. Lord for two reasons:

1. His credit was the victim of a recent identity theft, and some judgments that did not belong to him were on his credit record; and
2. Dr. Lord could not get insurance on one of his buildings because of a recent fire. This building held the majority of the equity.

Well, Dr. Lord contacted me, and we set up a Nevada corporation with full nominee officer and director protection. Then, his corporation entered into a loan agreement with each of his LLCs. In exchange for a $1,500,000 line of credit, his corporation filed a lien against each of the buildings. *(Our earlier example of Adrian utilized this cross-collateralization technique with a commercial lender for his two homes.)* Did Dr. Lord's corporation have $1,500,000? No way. In fact, it had less than $10,000, but the sharks lurking around Dr. Lord had no way of knowing this. To the sharks, Dr. Lord borrowed $1,500,000 and his Nevada Corporation with nominee officer and director protections has a secured interest in Dr. Lord's apartment buildings. By now you should realize that if Dr. Lord's Corporation does not loan the money to his LLCs, then the equity would still be available in the event of a lawsuit. Furthermore, you must be aware that you should never use this strategy to get a second mortgage on your properties. There have been a few recent cases where someone has used this strategy to persuade a bank to loan them additional capital to pay off their second mortgages. This is fraud, and it will have dire consequences for you if this strategy is used in this manner.

One last comment you may be thinking, "What happens if Dr. Lord wants to sell or refinance in the future; won't the lien affect his credit?" No. Why? Dr. Lord is not going to report his friendly lien to accredited reporting agencies, and he will remove the lien. So who is in control? Dr. Lord.

Thus, you need anonymity in your plan for the long run, and someone who knows how to do it right.

# Land Trusts—
*Privacy Plus Protection Equals Profit*

CHAPTER 4

For some people, the word "trust" implies a lot of money, or a big inheritance. In reality, a trust is a savvy way to protect your real estate investment, and to avoid many of the threats to real property that other forms of ownership don't allow. It is simply a system that allows one person (the trustee) to hold property for another (the beneficiary) and to perform certain duties. In the case of a land trust (sometimes known as an "Illinois-type" trust), a piece of real estate property is held by the trustee, but without any required duties attached. The main goal of a land trust—in most cases—is to remove your name from real estate property, so that if your assets are ever questioned or investigated, you remain anonymous.

Land trusts have been around for more than 500 years, and, like most aspects of law, the rules of land trust originate from merry old England. Under the feudal system, property generally passed automatically to the oldest son. However, ownership of the property hinged on military service and loyalty to the king, and included heavy taxation on the land. Some lawyers (yes, there were lawyers 500 years ago!) invented the land trust, which allowed the owner to transfer his interest in the land to a trusted someone (a trustee) to hold it for the beneficiary (the owner himself). In this way, an owner could sidestep many of the legal and financial obligations that accompanied owning real property.

Unsurprisingly, the monarchy wasn't happy with the arrangement. In 1536, King Henry VIII passed the Statute of Uses, which was tended to divert the booming land trust business. The Statute of Uses stated that when the land was placed with a trustee, the "use was executed" and the land went right back to the beneficiary. In other words, a land trust was useless and could easily be broken. Eight years later, after much litigation, the English courts amended the Statute of Uses, making it applicable only to passive trusts, trusts where the trustee had no legal or business duties.

Since American law still follows English precedent, a passive trust is void in most states. In many cases, this is written into the state statute. However, there are many states, such as Illinois and Florida and a handful of others, that offer broader regulations for land trusts, and that allow passive trusts where the trustee has some minor or nominal duty—such as signing a document every twenty years. In these states, the land trust is a very useful and simple tool even when the trustee has little to actually do. However, each state has different requirements—some require a simple signature, while others require a witness. Run afoul of these procedures and your entire trust could be completely void in a court of law. Here's an example of how land trusts can work.

> Toby owns a four-plex in Springfield, Illinois. His investment advisor suggests that he create a land trust to gain some privacy, but Toby thinks that sounds too complicated and sneaky, as if he has something to hide. He keeps his name as owner of the property, but plans to just stay out of sight of the tenants. Two years later, a fire starts from a faulty heating system. Toby had hired a handyman, but the handyman hadn't done a good job. The tenants do a property search

and find out that Toby is the owner of the property. They also get a complete record of his other assets and plan a lawsuit. If Toby had created a land trust, then his privacy would have been protected and no one would have known the depth of Toby's pockets because Toby's name would not have been on the title. In other words, Toby's ownership would have been hidden behind a trust.

There are some who argue that land trusts allow people to commit fraud or engage in illegal acts. However, in most cases, the land trust is simply a way to ensure privacy for the property owner. This is particularly important in our litigation-happy society, where lawsuits have become a path to wealth for many people. Furthermore, the privacy offered by a land trust isn't absolute and can be voided if a lawsuit is filed, but remember—we plan so that hopefully we won't have to defend because there won't be a lawsuit. For example, in the above case, a court can still order Toby's attorney to disclose his name as the beneficiary of the land trust.

Those cases aside, a land trust is still probably the best initial and inexpensive protection you can give to your real property. A land trust can provide privacy benefits similar to a Nevada Corporation except we replace nominee officers and directors with a nominee trustee. A land trust allows you to transfer property more easily than the traditional deed method. A land trust allows a debtor to sell property without alerting people or lenders to the sale. Of course, the debtor can't lie about the prop-

*To obtain more information on the use of Land Trusts, go to www.andersonadvisors.com and register for a free Gold membership. Search our Video section for "Land Trusts" and you will find several videos on this useful entity.*

erty he owns under oath, even if it is under a land trust. Nor can the debtor, if questioned by his lender, hide the fact he sold the property via a land trust. But at least he's not obliged to disclose his dealings with his property up front! Again, the land trust isn't quite bullet-proof, because unlike other forms of business entities discussed in Chapter 6, the land trust does not protect the real estate it holds from personal judgments entered against the trust beneficiaries or the trust beneficiaries from judgments entered against the trust itself. But a land trust can be difficult to dismantle, and it can put off potential litigants or creditors who don't understand this tool nor want the hassle of litigating against it.

> Marco decides to buy a condo in San Diego and consults with a local financial planner. He has heard that land trusts are a good asset protection solution, but the financial planner tells him that California doesn't have a land trust statute and therefore doesn't recognize land trusts. Marco wonders if he should get a second opinion—perhaps from a lawyer.

Marco is getting some bad advice from a financial planner who clearly doesn't know the law very well. It's true that many states don't have a land trust statute and don't formally recognize that term. However, that doesn't mean land trusts aren't valid in those states, such as California. Far from it—land trusts are valid in every state, even when not formally codified by law. Marco's financial planner may know the tax benefits of asset protection, but he certainly doesn't know the law. Remember—you need to know both.

## CONSTRUCTING A LAND TRUST

A land trust is a type of grantor trust *(which is the phrase you should use in states that don't formally recognize land trusts via statute)*. There are many types of grantor trusts, including living trusts and personal property trusts, all with generally the same purpose: to shift the title of property out of your name and into the care of a trustee.

How does a land trust work? There are three basic parties involved:

- **The Grantor**: This person sets up the trust and transfers assets into the trust.
- **The Trustee**: The person who manages the trust. The trustee should have actual duties so the trust isn't a passive trust. However, the grantor can name himself trustee if he wants to, but I recommend using another person. Of course you must trust that person. I will cover this later.
- **The Beneficiary**: The beneficiary is usually the grantor—he gets the "beneficial interest", i.e. ownership, of the trust.

The grantor deeds the property to the land trust; the trust agreement lists the name of the trustee(s) and the beneficiary(ies) of the trust. It's as simple as that. Of course, if the grantor, beneficiary, and trustee are all one person, the chief value of the trust—anonymity—is gone. So it's advisable that the trustee be someone other than the grantor. Here's how it works:

> Marco sets up the 675 Evergreen Trust, dated November 1, 2008, with himself as the trustee. When Marco deeds his property out of his name and into his trust, Marco will remain on public record because the property is titled in his trust as follows: Marco as Trustee of the 675 Evergreen Trust, dated November 1, 2008.

Marco's trust lacks one of the principle benefits of land trusts—anonymity. Even though Marco recorded his property under the

675 Evergreen Trust, his name still appears on the property's title as a trustee. Most people would assume that Marco created a trust for his own benefit, most likely, a personal living trust. If Marco had sought advice from an asset protection specialist familiar with land trust, he most likely would have been told to use a nominee trustee as his initial trustee.

The nominee trustee is a person, whom you trust, to serve as trustee for recording purposes only. After your property has been deeded from your personal name to that of the trust, which as I indicated includes the name of the trustee, your nominee trustee will resign and you will take control as the undisclosed successor trustee and the public will be left with the impression, because your name is no longer on the title, that you no longer own the property.

By way of reference, this is how the land trust is similar to a Nevada corporation with nominee officer and director protections. When I create a Nevada corporation, an attorney in my office assumes the initial director and officer position of the client's corporation. As the initial officer and director, the attorney's information is provided to the Nevada Secretary of State to be made public to anyone with a computer. After the initial filings are complete, control of the corporation is passed to my client with the nominee's resignation and my client's subsequent assumption of these positions. From the public's perspective, John Q attorney is listed as the nominee officer and director, and my client's involvement is hidden. This process can be repeated on a yearly basis to keep your involvement private.

When the trustee resigns, does this imply that your trust will be without a trustee? Absolutely not! When you create your trust, you will be sure to nominate successor trustees to assume control when the initial trustee is no longer serving. Who will be the successor trustee? You.

The question you might be asking of yourself at this point is what happens if your nominee trustee will not resign or, even worse, he sells your property. For me to answer these questions satisfactorily, you must understand the legal relationship between the trustee and the trust beneficiaries. How can the beneficiary fire the trustee who presumably has control? Most financial planners and attorneys you speak to about land trusts typically get this wrong. They do not understand this very important dynamic that distinguishes the land trust from a living trust. The trustee in a land trust holds title to trust property for the benefit of the trust beneficiaries. A trustee's powers are limited to the specific powers conferred to him under the trust agreement. All other powers are specifically reserved to the trust beneficiaries. In a good land trust agreement, your trustee should have the power to deal with tenants, make repairs, and expedite other limited expenditures, but all other matters concerning title, i.e. sale, loans, encumbrances, change in trustee, etc., require the consent of the trust beneficiaries. In other words, the beneficiaries are the ones with the real power under a land trust, which is why you should always be the beneficiary of any trust that holds title to your property.

*Free AP Lawyer Advice: Use extreme caution when choosing a nominee trustee. A client of mine elected to use a close friend who ended up having tax problems. Unfortunately for my client, his trustee's tax problems became my client's problem when New York state filed a tax lien on all trust property where the friend was listed as a trustee.*

What happens in the event your trustee turns out to be a rogue and sells the trust property without your consent? This exact question was put to me by a client's wife after she learned that her husband, the trustee of their land trust, sold the trust property without her involvement. Let me put that a different way: The wife knew the husband was going to sell the property but believed she would need to sign some paperwork to effectuate the sale.

To make matters worse, the husband had consulted an attorney who assisted with the closing and told the husband that he had full power of conveyance as the trustee of the trust. Wow, that was a huge mistake for an attorney to reach such a conclusion without reviewing the trust agreement. You see, in my trust agreement, it states . . . *Except as otherwise specifically provided in this trust agreement, all powers of the Trustee are subject to the consent of the Beneficiaries,* . . . . The trust then goes on to state that the Trustee can convey title to real property but only after he has obtained the beneficiaries' consent. So how does this alleviate the wife's concern? Simple, the trust beneficiaries could set the sale aside because they did not give their consent to the sale. The trustee will find himself embroiled in a lawsuit or two, and if an attorney gave the trustee his blessing and advice to move forward with the sale, then he will get the pleasure of experiencing the justice system from the other side of the table as well.

Another question I often receive is: Can my corporation be the trustee of my land trust? Yes, but with some caveats. To my knowledge, only Florida specifically authorizes a corporation, absent other requirements, to serve as the trustee of a land trust. Other states are silent on the issue, or specifically state that the corporation must be bonded and licensed in the state where the trust property resides. This can be a problem for those hoping to avoid jurisdictional issues. If you decide to proceed anyway, here's an example of how it can be used against you:

> Bob, an inexperienced attorney, establishes a land trust for his rental properties in Washington, with his corporation, NOIDEA, Inc., as the trustee. When a faulty balcony collapses resulting

in severe injuries to a tenant, Bob is sued. The tenant's attorney is quick to point out that NOIDEA, Inc., is not bonded and licensed in Washington, and that Bob is simply thumbing his nose at the law. Bob has given the Court one more reason to not like him—he is an attorney who doesn't know the law. Bob would be wise to settle.

## WHY INVESTORS USE LAND TRUSTS

Now you may be asking—how is the land trust going to help me? The answer lies in why the land trust was created, and why it's perfectly legal. It's basically a compromise between two opposing forces. On one side is the bank which is interested in generating income from loans and at the same time protecting itself through a security interest in real property—on the other side is the borrower (real property owner) who desires to transfer title to his property without fear of foreclosure or forced refinancing. The bank acts as the protagonist by incorporating a due-on-sale clause into most, if not all, mortgages its writes. The due-on-sale clause essentially means that the bank can decide to call in or accelerate its loan if the title of the property is ever transferred to another person or entity. This is important to real estate investors who desire asset protection or freedom of contract. If an investor wants to purchase property from a distressed seller subject to an existing mortgage, or to transfer his three properties into a limited liability company for asset protection, he does so at the risk that the lender discovers the transfers and subsequently accelerates the loans on the properties. Many investors are troubled by this potential outcome and, thus, elect not to protect their encumbered investment real estate.

Now in reality, I've met thousands of investors at my workshops, and in all the years I've done them I've only heard of one or two instances where the bank used the due-on-sale clause to force a person to refinance their loan. In these instances, the problem was simply that the owner was behind on his payments. But the due-on-sale clause has more ramifications than refinancing.

The bank's decisions are influenced primarily by economic forces, so it doesn't matter to them whether they are forcing you to refinance or not. Furthermore, the bank is probably not going to hold on to your mortgage. In the typical scenario, the bank will sell and resell mortgages to other banks as they need to. Of course, they won't allow homeowners to buy residences in entities or agree to the sale of real estate subject to an existing mortgage without first paying the mortgage in full. Why? Because if the bank attempts to sell the mortgage, a purchaser is not going to be willing to pay top dollar if they have to investigate who owns the property or the owners' credit rating. If the homeowner is forced to use his own name, then the bank and the potential purchaser of the mortgage have no problem doing business, since all the information is right there.

*Even though the Garn St. Germain Act stops banks from accelerating your mortgage, it does not prevent them charging a title transfer fee if you deed your property into a trust. Before signing a mortgage, be on the lookout for this sneaky provision that could end up costing you money if you deed your property into a trust.*

But from the homeowner's perspective, this is horrifying—and rightfully so. Not only is the homeowner forced to borrow money from a faceless lending corporation, he has no control over whom they sell the deed to, and who might enforce that due-on-sale clause. Even worse than that, he can't protect himself in terms of liability by purchasing his real estate investment with a limited liability entity, because most commercial lending institutions refuse to do business with entities unless the buyer agrees to pay commercial interest rates.

This nightmarish scenario is averted with the Garn St. Germain Act. This 1982 legislation had many goals, including making home mortgages available to a large number of people. The Garn St. Germain Act addresses the basic conflict between homeowners looking to protect their assets, and the bank's insistence that the homeowner buy the property in their own name. It prevents lenders from enforcing the due-on-sale clause when residential properties are transferred into a revocable trust and there is no change to the rights of occupancy. The key word here is revocable. Remember that a land trust is a revocable grantor trust that, as such, is covered under the Act.

Thus, under the Garn St. Germain Act an investor can create a land trust to hold title to his rental real estate without fear of his lender calling the mortgage due and payable. Once the property is held by the land trust, an investor has the flexibility to assign his beneficial interest to a limited liability company or another purchaser without alerting any third parties to the fact there has been a transfer. There are limits to the Garn St. Germain Act. If you have a property with more than four housing units, or have a loan that is not federally backed, then the Garn St. Germain Act does not apply.

## SITUATIONS WHERE AN INVESTOR SHOULD AVOID USING A LAND TRUST

Land trusts do not work for every type of property or situation that might arise during a person's investing career. Although situations may vary from state to state, here are a few examples you should be aware of before using this tool:

> Leigh Anne, a retired teacher, buys a studio apartment in Los Angeles. She sets up an Illinois-type land trust, with herself as the

grantor and the beneficiary, and her accountant as the trustee. Because this is an Illinois-type trust, she assigns virtually no duties to her CPA. When she decides to sell her property, she is shocked to find that the Illinois-type land trust isn't valid in California. In Illinois, it's possible to assign a trustee with no duties, but in California it's leaving you wide open to the Merger Doctrine which holds that a transfer does not take place when a trustee has no duties under the trust agreement. To remedy her mistake, Leigh Anne assigns an asset protection specialist as her trustee, and assigns him limited but very real duties.

Mark owns three properties in Miami, including a beachfront condominium. One day a fire starts in the heating vent, and a renter decides to sue. Mark, however, is savvy and holds the property in a land trust. He is the beneficiary and his attorney is the trustee. The renter discovers that Mark is the beneficiary, and names him as the defendant and landlord. Mark is confused: Isn't his land trust supposed to protect him? He consults with an attorney with experience in land trusts, who tells him his mistake: After setting up the land trust, Mark should have created an LLC and made it the beneficiary. That way the LLC, not Mark, would be held liable in the suit, since plaintiffs usually go after the beneficiary. Now, of course, it's too late as he's already been named in the suit.

Greg purchases an investment house in Houston. He sets up a land trust, naming himself as the grantor, Profit Wise, Inc., are the trustee, and Acme LLC as the beneficiary (both being entities that he owns). A few years later, a tenant in the property is severely burned when the electrical wiring, overloaded by a space heater, ignites the house. His asset protection specialist tells him he should have no problem, because he does not own the land trust but rather it is owned by his LLC. But when the lawsuit fires up, he finds out that Texas does not permit an entity to serve as a Trustee unless is it licensed and bonded. Greg's corporation is neither. Greg made a critical mistake that could jeopardize his asset protection.

As you can see, the land trust is a useful, simple tool to protect your property, but there are numerous variations in the protection that a land trust offers. There are many legal implications to consider; thus, you should have someone who knows the ins and outs of land trusts advise you. Otherwise, a land trust can offer no protection at all.

In the first example, Leigh Anne was worried about the due-on-sale clause and the idea that the bank could accelerate her loan when she tried to sell the property. However, her first mistake was not knowing the land trust laws of the state she lives in. Illinois has very generous land trust provisions, but many other states—especially those without codified land trust statutes—require that the trustee have actual duties and obligations. In Illinois, the trustee can do virtually nothing and the land trust is still protected, but this is not the case in California.

In Mark's case, he was savvy—he set up the land trust according to the rules of his state, with a trustee he could count on. However, he forgot one thing: While commercial lenders required that Mark buy the property in his own name, and perhaps also that Mark use his own name as beneficiary once he sets up the land trust, Mark is certainly not obliged to remain the beneficiary on paper. If he had transferred his beneficial interest into an LLC (also called an assignment), then the renter would not be going after him, but after the LLC. And if the LLC only holds this one asset, then Mark's money and his other properties are all safe.

Greg, on the other hand, thought he was doing everything by the book, but he forgot one aspect of asset protection: Know your state laws. When he transferred property into his land trust, he was unaware of Texas' legal requirements regarding an entity that serves as a trustee of a trust. This simple mistake has the potential to dismantle his entire plan.

There are numerous other advantages to land trusts. First, the transfer of property is much easier in a land trust than in an LLC or virtually any other corporate entity. With a land trust, if you want to transfer your rights to the property to another person, you simply assign them as beneficiary. It's as simple as that! The transfer of title doesn't make the bank or your creditors suspicious because the sale or transfer of your beneficial interest is not a public record. Thus, if no one is alerted to the transfer, then it is unlikely the bank will accelerate the mortgage.

A land trust, in this way, also avoids probate, which is the court proceeding after someone dies. A will is complicated, requires an attorney, witnesses, and a particular format and language. A land trust is simple; instead of a will, the owner can simply name a new beneficiary to the trust, and avoid all the trouble and wasted time of probate. Transferring interests is simple for a land trust, and therefore gives the owner of the property a great deal of control.

A land trust offers privacy in terms of transferring interests. With a land trust, unlike a conventional purchase and sale of property, issues such as the sale price and details of transfer are not on public record. The land trust also allows the beneficiary to report his equity interest in the property on his financial statement—without reporting the mortgage. Why? Because as the beneficiary, you own the equity interest in a property as an asset, but are not required to report the mortgage as a liability, because that is an obligation (liability) of the trust.

As you can see, the land trust offers a great deal of protection for the real estate investor. Given the infinite number of problems that a real estate investor faces, the land trust is a smart solution to keeping control over the property, avoiding the risk of litigation and tax liability, and protecting both rental properties and homesteads.

Below is a list of states with codified land trust statutes—meaning that there are laws that regulate how land trusts work. In other states without codified land trust statues, land trusts are still legal, but the rules regarding them are interpreted by common law—or court rulings and precedent. Virtually every state has some type of law on the books that deals with land trusts in the state. In all cases, you should talk to an asset protection specialist to figure out the ins and outs of your state laws on land trusts.

### States with Land Trust Statutes or Laws on Land Trusts

Florida
Georgia
Hawaii
Illinois
North Carolina
North Dakota
Virginia

In those states without land trust laws on the books, transferring your property to a living, revocable trust can provide exactly the same benefits. It's also important to note that unlike an LLC or other corporate entity, a land trust does not have to be assigned to a particular state or jurisdiction.

When it comes to land trusts, there's a lot of uncertainty since they're not formally recognized everywhere. The law changes all the time, and your case might bring brand new issues before the court. I tell my clients that it's better not to bring any new issues on the table, and to not make themselves more vulnerable than they already are.

## ISSUES WITH LAND TRUSTS

Having heard so much about the benefits of the trusts, you may be ready to set one up. That's fine; land trusts are extremely useful in many ways. However, there are many drawbacks to land trusts as well.

First, there's the fact that while the land trust offers anonymity and allows transfers to be done easily, it offers little to offset actual litigation or taxes. In the course of litigation, it can be very easy to trace how a land trust was created, thereby eliminating your anonymity, and, if litigation is successful, then you as the trust beneficiary will be personally liable. That's why it's important that the beneficiary be an LLC rather than you personally.

Second, because a land trust isn't recognized by statute in every state, many lenders, insurance brokers, and mortgage specialists are reluctant to get involved with them. It can also be hard to get a full homestead exemption in some states that aren't equipped to deal with the trust.

Third, there are some legal issues at stake, specifically the fact that the trustee does not need to perform any duties. This means that the equitable title and the legal title merge. What does this mean without the legalese? Well, it basically means that the title of the person doing the work (the trustee) and the title of the person getting the benefit (the beneficiary) cover essentially the same job. If the trustee has absolutely nothing to do, then it can be difficult to persuade a court that your land trust is a valid entity. However, there are a few states that clearly allow a trustee to have virtually no duties.

Finally, there are some arguments that land trusts enable fraud. Apart from the possibility that masking the ownership of a property will lead to masking criminal behavior, there's also the issue of the timing of transfers. A court could find that if a land trust was set up with intent to commit fraud, it is invalid, and that the property is therefore available to creditors.

The main advantage of a land trust, and the main reason to set one up, goes back to the title of this chapter: You want to look like you qualify for food stamps. When a creditor or potential litigant looks up your name, he should see that you have virtually no assets, and therefore are not worth pursuing. A land trust takes care of the largest problem in that strategy—real property. By putting your home or rental property in another name, you are defending yourself against potential threats to your assets. The land trust, therefore, is a primary weapon of the real estate investor and the small business owner.

But while a land trust is a valuable tool, it provides no help on your tax returns or in the event of an actual lawsuit. This is where business entities come in. I've been talking about them all along—corporations, limited partnerships, and limited liability companies—but in the next chapter, we'll discuss all the variations. You don't have to be a millionaire to set up a business entity, but you do need to know which entity is appropriate for your given business. It will be a relatively painless overview; your asset protection specialist is the one who really needs to know the nitty gritty and the legalese involved.

# Comparison of Business Entities—
## *Striking a Balance between Assets Protection and Taxation*

Whenever I begin an asset protection discussion with someone who has not attended one of my workshops, it always starts with a brief overview of liability protection versus asset protection. The difference between these concepts can radically impact the plan you put together, especially when you add taxation into the mix.

### LIABILITY PROTECTION

Liability protection is a concern to any person who conducts an activity that has the potential to create either physical or monetary harm to another person. Here's an example:

> Ben owns several residential properties that he actively manages. Ben's duties typically include renting, evicting, and proper maintenance of his properties. One winter, after a blistering ice storm, Ben decides to salt the walkways on each of his properties. On the last property, Ben runs out of salt. Running late for a dinner date, Ben decides to finish the job the

next morning. Unfortunately for Ben, not twenty minutes after his departure, Susan, a tenant who is six months pregnant, slipped and fell on the unsalted portion of the walkway. Susan suffered a broken back and multiple fractures, and the status of her unborn baby is guarded.

The potential damages from such a suit could easily wipe Ben out, leaving him without any properties to manage. Now Ben might have prevented his complete financial collapse by forming an entity that protected him and his investments. This form of protection is what asset protection specialists commonly refer to as liability protection. Liability protection planning is the act of creating a business entity that protects you as an individual from the liabilities associated with the business. Ben's business was property management, and Ben conducted this business activity as a sole proprietor. In other words, Ben managed his properties in his own name. As the property manager, Ben was responsible for the tenants' safety. Ben breached his duty when he failed to salt the walkway, which thereby resulted in Susan's injuries.

Ben might have avoided personal liability if he had created a corporation to manage his properties. If a corporation were the property manager, then Susan would be forced to look to Ben's corporation for recovery rather than to Ben individually. In other words, Ben's corporation is liable to Susan but Ben as an individual is not.

Liability protection is not all that Ben needs. Ben owns the property where Susan was injured. Susan could elect to sue Ben in addition to his property management corporation. Ben cannot hide behind the property manager, because Ben, as the owner of the property where the harm occurred, is ultimately responsible for injuries that befall his tenants. When Susan puts her sights on Ben, all of his investments will be at risk because Ben owns everything in his own name. Ben is also in need of asset protection.

To protect Ben, a good attorney might recommend that Ben place each of his rentals in an entity that removes the property and the entity itself beyond the reach of Ben's personal creditors. Entities that perform this function are referred to as asset protection entities because they protect your assets from your personal liabilities and you from your assets' liabilities.

You should see by now that the first thing every real estate investor needs to understand is how the various corporate entities can help protect your investment, and keep your property safe from legal and tax liabilities. I've discussed corporations and limited liability companies (LLC) before in a general way, but that's just scraping the surface of business organizations. It may seem daunting to realize how many different business entities there are and how many advantages and disadvantages there are to each. However, a well-structured asset protection plan is the answer to effectively protecting and managing your real estate assets, whether you own a fleet of skyscrapers or just one condominium. And, once you get the hang of it, business entities start making intuitive sense.

## THE CORPORATION

The most traditional type of business organization, besides the sole proprietorship, is the corporation. A corporation is a separate, free-standing legal entity that I often refer to as an artificial person that you control. Think of it as a robot you program to conduct your business, but if anything goes wrong the robot gets the blame. Doesn't this sound great? It should. Corporations are by far the most widely used entity to conduct business because of the liability protections it provides for its owners, officers, and directors, in addition to the numerous tax benefits specifically bestowed on this form of business entity. In my workshops, I have found that much confusion surrounds the players in the corporation and their interaction vis-à-vis each other and the corporation. What most people don't grasp is that these are just positions with different functions. Think of it as building a house. The owner (shareholder) puts up the money and hires a general contractor (director) to build the house. The owner knows that the general contractor is not going to build the house himself, but that he is going to hire subcontractors (officers) to perform the various aspects of the construction. These subcontractors will bring with them their own crews (employees) to perform the majority of the heavy lifting.

Which positions will you hold? How about all three—shareholder, director, and officer? Through a corporation, you can buy, sell, rehab, develop, and manage real estate. It can pay the salaries, borrow or loan money—literally anything you can do as a person can be done through a corporation—but with one major exception, when done through a corporation you have liability protection. Shareholders, directors, and officers are typically shielded from most liabilities.

Many people have preconceived notions that corporations are for big business and without tons of capital and at least several people the corporation is not an option. This is incorrect, and as a result of this thinking many people miss out on the benefits a corporation can provide its owners.

Another area of confusion surrounds the type of corporations that are available. There is only one type of corporation, although most people I meet are convinced that two types exist: "C" corporations and "S" corporations. In reality C and S refer to the tax code and have nothing to do with the actual corporate form.

A C corporation is the more traditional type of entity, and has the advantage of a fiscal year-end, increased deductions, and a reduced dividend tax rate of 15% (increasing to 20% in 2011 under present law). That means that the corporation pays a corporate tax on its profits, then pays dividends to its shareholders, who then pay a flat tax of 15% on the income. In some situations this can be advantageous, or it can result in high taxes overall, depending on the business.

An S-type corporation can be more tax friendly, as it essentially allows the corporation's profits to pass directly on to the shareholders, who then pay taxes (so taxes are paid only once on the total corporation income). It's easy to see how big a difference this could make if you've set up a corporation to save money on your real estate properties, only to have to pay taxes on both your corporation and your personal tax returns! There is little difference in the tax filing for an S Corporation compared with a C, only an additional form you submit after your corporation is filed, whereupon you elect S-Corporation treatment.

## LIMITED PARTNERSHIP

Another common form of business entity used by many individuals for its excellent asset protection qualities is the limited partnership (LP). The vast majority of people I meet have heard of this entity, albeit in its more general parlance referred to as the family limited partnership. To be legally correct, a family limited partnership does not exist. The term *family limited partnership* is a pseudonym for limited partnership, which many attorneys and accountants have adopted to help their clients develop a mental connection between the limited partnership and the protection of family assets.

Why all the excitement over this entity? It is best understood if we back up a bit and examine the nuances of a general partnership, which will then make the limited partnership benefits abundantly clear.

*To obtain more information on the different business forms go to www.andersonadvisors.com, register for a free Gold membership then search our Video section for "Business Structuring 101" to view a detailed comparison of business forms.*

A general partnership is similar to a sole proprietorship with one important difference. In a sole proprietorship, there can be only one business owner—hence the term *sole*, meaning "one". A general partnership exists when there is more than one individual owning a business venture. This association of individuals conducting a business venture is governed by state statute (the Uniform Partnership Act—adopted by most states), but it does not require formal legal recognition. In other words, you are not required to file articles of organization or to adopt a written partnership operating agreement. This form of business arrangement is extremely dangerous because it lacks both liability protection and asset protection for its owners.

> Consider Mac, Kyle, and Peter who decide to jump into rehabbing properties under the name Quality Home Sellers. Each of them puts up $30,000, and together they purchase their first property at auction. Unfortunately for the three of them, Mac and Kyle each have different ideas on rehabbing property. Mac wants to go upscale, while Kyle believes that cheaper is better. Unbeknownst to Kyle or Peter, Mac contracts with several local building material suppliers for granite counters, hardwood floors, and professional quality appliances. Meanwhile, Kyle is busy replacing all of the electrical himself. Both partners are making decisions without the consent or knowledge of the other partners. After the property is sold, the adventure truly begins for these investors.

Each partner receives a bill from the various suppliers demanding more than $80,000 for the materials Mac ordered. Kyle and Peter are furious with Mac because he did not get their consent for the purchases. To make matters worse, due to Peter's use of the wrong gauge electrical wire, a fire started that severely burned one of the homeowners. Upon hearing about the fire, Mac and Peter fled to Mexico.

This brief story exemplifies the potential problems faced by many real estate investors. You know the saying "Look before you leap!" Well, these individuals didn't follow this advice and chose not to consult an asset protection specialist before they began their investing. Most people approach a new business undertaking with the belief that they need to make some money before seeking business and asset protection advice. As you can gather, this mindset cost Mac, Kyle, and Peter everything, and here's why.

Mac, Kyle, and Peter are considered a general partnership under the law because the three of them joined together to conduct a business venture. As a general partnership, each of them is subject to joint and several liability. This means that together or separately the partners can be held to answer to the creditors of the partnership. In the example, Peter was completely unaware of Mac and Kyle's activities; however, ignorance is no excuse under the law, and Peter will have to answer for the fire and the purchases even though he was not involved in either. All of Peter's assets are at risk. Mac and Kyle escaped and left their friend Peter to clean up the mess. Because of the unlimited liability exposure in general partnerships, the limited partnership evolved as a tool to reduce the liability exposure of partners like Peter who are not involved in the business' decision-making processes. Peter wanted to profit from real estate but not participate in the day-to-day business, while

Mac and Kyle wanted both. These divergent interests comprise the basic structure of a limited partnership.

A limited partnership consists of two classes of partners, general and limited. Each class has different rights and liabilities that are derived from state law, but which in many instances can be modified by a written partnership agreement. The general partner in a limited partnership is the decision maker. The general partner controls all aspects of the limited partnership's business, including when, if, and how the other partners receive partnership profits. In exchange for control, a general partner must sacrifice asset protection and assume unlimited liability for all of the limited partnership obligations. In a limited partnership, control comes with a heavy price.

On the other hand, a limited partner has no control over the management of the limited partnership. Limited partners must rely on the general partner to make sound business decisions and trust that the general partner will distribute partnership profits on occasion. In exchange for conceding control to the general partner, a limited partner is protected against partnership obligations. The only risk a limited partner faces is the loss of his investment.

If Quality Home Sellers was formed as a limited partnership, it should be fairly obvious that Mac and Kyle would be considered general partners and Peter a limited partner. As a limited partner, Peter would have been insulated from the lawsuits brought by the material suppliers and the injured homeowner. Peter's total exposure would be capped at his $30,000 investment in the limited partnership. Mac and Kyle's situation, on the other hand, would be a different story, and upon their return from Mexico, each of them would be staring down the barrel of two expensive lawsuits.

You should understand that a person or a business entity could be both a limited partner and a general partner in a limited partnership. The reason for being a general partner is obvious—control, but the solution to the control-in exchange-for-liability-protection dilemma is not. Every real estate investor who understands the liabilities he faces wants asset protection, but at the same time he understands that he can't run his business if he does not have control. To work around this problem, the smart money is on using a corporation as the general partner and the real estate investor as a limited partner.

The corporation will shield you from the liability associated with serving as a general partner, and as a limited partner you enjoy the favorable flow-through tax treatment associated with partnerships. This time-tested strategy has served investors well, but for many people the thought of using two entities to run their investing seems like overkill. An alternative was desired—one that provided all of the benefits of the limited partnership without the added work of utilizing two entities. In response to pleas, a new entity was crafted in 1977, what is commonly known as the limited liability company (LLC).

## LIMITED LIABILITY COMPANY

Limited liability companies have become far and away the most popular entity for small to medium-sized businesses. The chief reason for their popularity lies in the LLC's unique combination of asset protection benefits equal to limited partnerships, coupled with the liability protections and flexibility of corporations. These combined features allow you to invest in a business, exercise control, and maintain asset protection. You can even form an LLC with only one member and dispense with the rigid business formalities associated with corporations.

This sounds great! Everyone should have an LLC, you have probably been told, because they are so simple to create and the benefits are plentiful. In fact, many professionals I know recommend this form of business entity to their clients. Unfortunately, this process is not as simple as some would like you to believe. I have met countless real estate investors and business owners who, upon the recommendation of a friend, seminar speaker, attorney, or website, have made the decision to create an LLC for their business without understanding the why behind the entity creation instead preferring to follow the lead of others who obviously did the thinking for them. Sound a bit harsh? It should. I have asked hundred of people who created LLCs for their businesses the same four questions: Is your LLC member-managed or manager-managed? Why did you choose a particular management structure? How is your LLC taxed, and how will that affect you personally? The answers I received disturbed me:

> *Most people asked don't know if their LLC is member-managed or manager-managed, nor or why one form was chosen over another. When it comes to taxation, almost everyone is at a loss because taxation, like management structure, was never discussed during the planning phase of their entity.*

These questions are extremely important, because the decisions you make can impact your overall asset protection plan and how much you will pay in taxes.

In a member-managed LLC, each member has a say in the business decisions and future goals of the LLC. While this is certainly the most egalitarian way to go, it can get really complicated if you have more than just a few members. A regular member meeting could still keep things organized, but that makes the LLC very similar to a corporation, with its required shareholder meeting and other strict procedures. But an even more important question to ask yourself when forming an LLC is: Do you want everyone to have control?

It is my personal belief that when forming an LLC with multiple members, it may not be wise to give control to the membership. I have had many attorneys tell me that this is a non-issue for their clients because all the current members will be the decision makers, so a member-managed LLC makes perfect sense. Consider the following:

> Dave and Sue, through their attorney, establish a member-managed LLC to hold two rental properties. Several years later, on the advice of their attorney, Dave and Sue gift 40% of their LLC membership interests to their two children, ages 18 and 20, for income and estate tax planning reasons.

Do you notice a problem with this picture? Dave and Sue are now sharing control of two very valuable properties with their children because the children are now members and the members have management control. When I raise this issue with attorneys or CPAs, I am told they would change the LLC's management structure from member-managed to manager-managed before the gift. Thus, I am left to wonder why set up a structure you know will most likely be changed in the future. Any answers come to mind? —how about additional attorney fees?

A manager-managed LLC vests control in one or more managers who may or may not be members. The principal advantage to this structure is the separation of control from ownership. In Dave and Sue's situation, they could comfortably transfer ownership interests to their children without relinquishing control of the company.

Another inherent drawback to member-managed LLCs is the lack of anonymity. For member-managed LLCs, every state requires that the members' names be disclosed, and this information is made available to the general public via the Secretary of State's website. As a real estate investor, I do not particularly relish the thought of my tenants knowing who owns the property in which they reside.

Many investors have surely experienced a disgruntled tenants' late-night harassing phone calls because they made the mistake of informing the tenant that they owned the property.

The innovative solution to this problem, if you haven't already guessed it, is to create a manager-managed LLC. In stark contrast to the member-managed LLC, with a manager-managed LLC the Secretary of State typically collects only the manager's information. Thus, each non-managing member's identity remains anonymous.

Taxation is another issue that is often overlooked when deciding to form an LLC. Unlike a corporation that can elect either C or S federal taxation treatment or a limited partnership that can only be taxed as a partnership, an LLC can elect any of the three, or, in the situation where a LLC has only one member, it can elect to be ignored for federal tax purposes. Disregarded tax status has many advantages for the real estate investor—the best part being fewer tax returns.

A disregarded LLC is similar to a pass-through entity like the limited partnership or a corporation that has elected S treatment, but unlike these entities, the disregarded LLC is completely ignored for federal tax purposes. In fact, the entity does not even file a federal tax return because the LLC's member is treated as owning the assets outright and not through an LLC. For asset protection purposes, the LLC is considered the owner, but for federal tax purposes the assets are considered to be owned by the LLC's member. The planning opportunities presented by this entity are extraordinary!

## SERIES LIMITED LIABILITY COMPANY

A variation on the LLC is the Series LLC, also known as the Delaware Series LLC, which, given sufficient time to be tested in the courts, could be particularly useful to real estate investors in the future. The Series LLC must be formed in a state such as Nevada or Delaware that statutorily recognizes this unique *form* of entity. It's similar to having multiple LLCs for different properties, but instead simplifies matters by allowing one LLC to operate numerous other subsidiary LLCs, each of which runs a single-asset business. For the real estate investor, this means that each subsidiary LLC owns one property, protecting it from the liability of the other properties, just as multiple corporate entities would do. The Series LLC could simplify things greatly: fewer forms, fewer reports, and a much easier way to manage multiple properties than if you had to form a new, independent LLC for each.

The Series LLC is potentially useful for owning and managing business properties, especially if the real estate in question is used for running a business. A business formed under a Series LLC could have one subsidiary LLC to own and manage the business property, while another LLC manages the assets and day-to-day business operations. The Series LLC also has increased ability to transfer assets between businesses, without incurring penalties or tax liability.

Some lawyers and asset protection consultants advise their customers to form Series LLCs, often without discussing the drawbacks. First, the Series LLC is new and has not been tested in terms of asset protection. Only a handful of states have adopted statutes recognizing this form of business entity, and because of its recent arrival on the business scene there are no court cases yet that determine how the Series LLC will be treated if one of the series comes under assault in a lawsuit. Second, there is a lot of uncertainty in the federal government about how the Series LLC should be taxed. Therefore, creating a Series LLC for real estate and asset protection purposes is still largely uncharted territory. There are guidelines for formation, but very little in the way of guidelines for governing business operations, taxation, or legal liability.

## TRUSTS

With so many business entities to choose from, it may surprise you that you can conduct your business without using any of them. In order to avoid probate, manage property for your dependents and beneficiaries, and reduce federal estate taxes, many investors choose a trust. As we have seen, trusts are particularly useful ways to deal with real property, as they allow for an easier transfer of assets than a corporate entity does. Basically, a trust involves three parties:

1. **The Trustor (or grantor):** who owns the property and holds it for the benefit of the—
2. **Beneficiary:** who owns legal title to the property, even though the trust is not in the beneficiary's name. The trust is managed by the—
3. **Trustee:** a trustworthy third party who administers the trust for the benefit of the beneficiary until the title finally transfers over.

This rather simple structure can have numerous hidden advantages. One trustor can have one trust for multiple successive beneficiaries, in case one beneficiary should die. In this way, an investor can make sure that his property passes on to his children, and to his children's children. Furthermore, there can be numerous trustors or even co-trustees. The main advantage of the trust is the transfer of assets to beneficiaries without getting hit by probate fees and expenses.

There are numerous types of trusts, which can be specific to the state you reside in. No investor should navigate the world of trusts alone. The following descriptions merely scratch the surface of trusts as an asset protection tool.

The offshore trust is probably the most famous—and infamous—of asset protection tools. An offshore trust is simply one that is administered and settled outside of the United States. The main requirement is that the jurisdiction of the trust—the country or region where the trust is established—formally recognizes the concept of the trust. As you may remember, not all states formally recognize trusts, but to have your trust established outside of the U.S. you need a country that either has trust laws or allows trusts to be administered by the trust laws of another country (for instance, the U.S.). Interestingly, for people outside the U.S. looking for trusts, America is one of the world's largest offshore jurisdictions.

An offshore trust has many general advantages. A location outside the United States can offer wide access to global markets and opportunities not available to U.S.-based investors. An offshore trust dealing with goods and services may pay fewer taxes than a U.S.-based trust trying to do business overseas. An offshore trust can place your assets beyond the reach of potential creditors because of the anonymity, complexity, and general barriers to collection generally afforded by these trusts and the jurisdiction where they are created.

Setting up an offshore trust is complex, and sometimes there exists a presumption of fraudulent intent on the grantor's part not to mention that you are dealing with a third world jurisdiction with little oversight and protections for your investments. Far too many people think an offshore trust is the best way to limit the threat of litigation, or limit taxes. Much "wink wink, nod nod" has gone on in the offshore trust arena, and as a result these trusts are instant red flags to the IRS. Improper setup and management of the trust can result in legal fines and penalties, which is why it is so important to have an asset protection specialist who knows what he's doing in this field, both legally and from a tax perspective.

Another useful type of trust is the irrevocable trust. An irrevocable trust (as opposed to a revocable one) is a trust that cannot be changed once it is set up. In some cases, changes can be made if the beneficiary allows it. An irrevocable trust is particularly useful when trying to transfer ownership of assets to a beneficiary without the beneficiary gaining control over the assets. With an irrevocable trust, a trustor can start giving away property and profits to his dependents with fewer tax consequences. In many cases, a trust that is created to avoid or reduce federal taxes is considered irrevocable upon the trustor's death, while a trust that is simply employed to avoid probate court is often revocable. It's important to note that it's not easy for the average investor to avoid both federal estate taxes and probate court with a trust.

A living trust may be revocable or irrevocable, depending on how it's set up. A living trust is simply a trust that transfers assets while the trustor is still alive. It operates differently from an irrevocable trust or a will because a living trust almost always avoids probate. Many of the land trusts discussed earlier are living trusts, and they are more useful than traditional wills since they can salvage the 5%–10% of your assets that might otherwise get eaten up in probate court.

What the trust can't do, however, is protect your property from creditors. A trust cannot shield you from legal liability. However, since a trust is not a matter of public record, it can be harder for a would-be litigator to figure out who owns the house, and whose assets are fair game. A trust requires certain forms of paperwork, and though many websites suggest doing it on your own, the right lawyer and asset protection specialist can make sure that there aren't any red flags in your holdings.

## NEVADA, DELAWARE, WYOMING —THE ORGANIZER'S DILEMMA

So which is right for you? Do you incorporate your rentals, or do you run your rehabbing business through an LLC? At first glance, it seems like both organization types are useful. However, there are some details specific to doing business in certain states that will affect which entity you need for which property.

Traditionally, Delaware has been home to the American corporation, with case law on corporate entities spanning more than a century. The laws tend to favor shareholders as opposed to management. Delaware is ideal for Fortune 500 companies who have shareholders they need to account to, but not for the smaller investor. For one thing, Delaware has both a state and a corporate tax. This means that your identity is not protected for asset protection purposes, and the corporation or LLC you have created must pay federal and Delaware state and corporate taxes. Delaware does not, however, charge a tax on the number of corporate shares. Companies forming in Delaware have no minimum capital requirements, and no limits on the stock or shares that can be issued.

Nevada, on the other hand, is a friend of the little guy. In recent years, Nevada has become the golden state for smaller investors who are looking to keep their property ownership quiet. Nevada does not reveal the identities of people who have created corporate entities, and it has no state, franchise, or corporate taxes. These benefits alone have propelled Nevada to becoming one of the best states of incorporation for small business owners. As if this wasn't enough, Nevada has also adopted some of the best asset protection laws in the country. In Nevada, the much-coveted charging order which protects you from personal creditors acquiring ownership of your business entities to satisfy a personal judgment (described

*Every Nevada entity should have a nexus to the State. Nexus gives your corporation legitimacy by providing a physical presence i.e., a Nevada business address and phone number. I highly recommend Business Office Suite Services in Nevada to serve as your business nexus. Go to www.bossoffice.com for more information on their valuable service.*

in detail in Chapter 6) applies not only to traditional entities such as LPs and LLCs, but as of 2007 those protections were extended to closely held corporations with fewer than 75 shareholders. Now it is possible to set up a complete structure for real estate investors that provides complete asset and liability protection.

However, I believe it is important to note that many promoters of Nevada tout bearer shares, stock issued to the holder of the certificate, and Nevada's lack of information-sharing with the IRS as other benefits worthy of incorporation. In my opinion, these benefits, if practiced by a business owner, will only result in future trouble and should never be relied upon for asset protection.

What has vaulted Nevada into its premiere position? In a word—privacy. Unlike the vast majority of other states, a corporation or LLC formed in Nevada can benefit from nominee protections. I briefly touched on this topic in Chapter 5 when discussing land trusts, but now it is time to do it justice so you can appreciate how valuable this can be in your asset protection structure.

> Roger and Norma decide to make the smart choice and form a corporation for their pre-foreclosure business in Texas. Roger and Norma consult a local attorney who rolls his eyes at Norma's suggestion that they form a Nevada corporation. After much discussion, Roger and Norma are cajoled into forming a

Texas corporation. Shortly after the corporation is established, Roger and Norma blanket two zip codes offering to buy homes for cash. After their third mailing, some recipients call the local newspaper to complain. The newspaper investigates the corporation through the Texas Secretary of State website and then runs an article naming Roger and Norma as the so-described "culprits" behind the mailings.

The problem in Roger and Norma's situation is twofold. First, they are working with an attorney who does not understand the importance of privacy. In fact, most attorneys do not understand it because privacy runs counter to how they market themselves—unless your idea of privacy is plastering your face on a billboard asking people to call you! The second problem is how most attorneys or CPAs approach business. Frankly, most will tell you they are not businessmen. You can test me on this by asking your local CPA or attorney if he considers himself to be a professional first or a businessman first. Hopefully you won't get billed for his answer, but you understand my point. If you are not accustomed to running a business, especially an active real estate business, you are not going to know what is important to your client's success. I can tell you this about Roger and Norma: They are starting over with a new attorney who gets the importance of privacy in an asset protection plan.

Nevada is the solution to the problem presented when Norma and Roger formed their corporation. In Nevada, experienced asset protection planners will always use a nominee officer and director when forming a corporation. Does this imply someone you don't know will be involved with your business? Absolutely not! The nominee officer and director are for filing purposes only. Like the LLC, which must disclose its manager, corporations must disclose their current officers and directors. In fact, if there is a change in these positions during the year, the state must be updated. In Nevada, they take a different approach. Nevada requires a corporation to disclose its current officers and directors once a year. In other words, you can appoint a third-party nominee to serve as your officer and director for filing purposes only. The nominee does not hold any tangible power over your business and is appointed in name only. After your filing is complete, the nominee resigns and you assume your officer and director positions. Thus, if someone looks up your corporation, they will not associate it with you. This process is repeated on a yearly basis to maintain your anonymity. Thereby casting your business in a pond of several thousand other entities utilizing a nominee. In fact, one of the attorneys in my firm is listed as a nominee on over 17,000 Nevada entities.

*If using a nominee officer and director it is prudent to select someone who is an attorney. Attorney's have insurance that will protect you if they act inappropriately vis-a-vis your corporation and should someone inquire about your corporation your attorney/nominee will refuse to disclose any information because of his attorney-client privilege.*

Just think of it this way: your personal business information should always be on a need-to-know basis, not a need-to-show basis, and is the approach to be taken in Norma and Roger's situation. One last point: Always use an attorney as your nominee for added protection.

Anonymity is very important when it comes to asset protection, but another area that sets Nevada apart from states that claim to offer similar protections is Nevada's business courts. As an attorney who occasionally finds himself in court, I find it extremely frustrating to have a judge who is unfamiliar with the legal topics presented. However, this should come as no surprise given the fact that in most states judges will rotate between civil and criminal courts, and, thus, never have the time to gain an expertise in one particular area. When it comes to asset protection, "certainty" is something to be desired. If the legal framework you are counting on for asset protection is challenged, you definitely want a judge well-versed in charging orders, director and officer protections, and shareholder issues presiding over your case. Nevada provides this level of protection.

*To appreciate how important a business court can be when adjudicating matters of asset protection, go to www.andersonadvisors.com and click on the "News" tab, then search for "Florida Supreme Court Debates" to read an interesting article that discusses how the Florida Supreme Court Justices do not know the difference between a limited liability company and a corporation.*

But Nevada and Delaware are not the last word on asset protection. In the last few years, Wyoming has emerged as a new state that's friendly to small business and corporations. Like Nevada, Wyoming has no tax on corporate shares, no limits on stock or shares issues, and no minimal capital requirements. And, like Nevada, Wyoming has no state corporate taxes and no franchise tax, allows nominee officers and directors, and does not reveal the names of company owners. Unlike Nevada, however, Wyoming does not extend charging order protections to its corporations.

As you can see, corporate entities are not too difficult to understand, but they are certainly no picnic to set up. Where you set one up and how can make or break your profit margin, and either keep you safe from or utterly exposed to the IRS and litigious tenants. In the next chapter, we'll specifically discuss asset protection for real estate properties, primarily using LLCs and corporations.

# Asset Protection for Real Estate—
*Insurance Is Not Your Only Option*

Many real estate investors don't know what they're getting into. It's easy to see a fixer-upper property and envision it with happy renters who pay on time, sending you an income for doing virtually nothing (once you have developed the property). It's easier still to envision a set of rental properties, all doing the same thing—generating positive cash flow. Even better, it doesn't take a lot of money to invest in real estate; however, it's certainly not as easy as it would appear. Here's an example:

> Adrian decides to invest his money in a small rental property near Central Park in New York City. He plans to keep most of the original tenants but fix up some of the top floor apartments to attract higher-end renters. Most of the tenants are pretty happy with the decision, until the construction goes on longer than planned. Soon, everyone wants a reduction in the rent because of their lowered quality of life. But the clincher is when the boy on the first floor is diagnosed with asthma, brought on by excessive exposure to crumbling plaster, paint, and brick dust. All bets are off, and suddenly Adrian finds himself in a lawsuit with the boy's mother, and

fighting to claim his rent from his once friendly tenants. So much for a safe investment.

When it comes to real estate, tenants and environmental liability are not the only problems. Real estate investors—especially those using small to medium-sized capital—run many risks when getting involved in the real estate market. For example, does Adrian charge the repairs to his credit card, or take out a bank loan? Should he incorporate or become an LLC, or continue to take the informal approach (such as with a sole proprietorship)? How long is he planning to hold the investment? This could affect the tax treatment and capital gains rates. Will he have to pay the asthmatic boy's medical expenses out of pocket? What happens if he gets taken to court? Adrian had only the best intentions—improving a rental property without upsetting the current tenants. But when it comes to people's homes, there's no sense in dealing with them informally. Even the friendliest tenant can easily turn on you, if the circumstances are right.

So—what are you going to do about it?

Adrian missed some crucial steps in his acquisition of the property. He saw an opportunity for easy money and figured he could do business and stay friendly with all the parties involved. All the potential technicalities that seemed too "nitpicky" are coming back to haunt him—as well as some that he had never considered. Since he did the whole deal out of his own pocket, he's going to be held liable for all the costs and the claims in any lawsuit. If Adrian had taken the time to consult an attorney or an asset protection specialist, he might have discovered some easy tricks to safeguard his assets and to save money on his remodeling, his legal costs, and his personal heartache. Instead, Adrian tried to do it himself—never a good idea!

All real estate investors face problems with tenants and with many issues related to the physical property itself: zoning, permits, plumbing, upkeep of general access areas and stairwells, individual complaints from apartment dwellers, and environmental and governmental standards and issues. It's no easy task facing these threats, so the real estate investor, whether looking for a short-term buy or a long-term rental, needs to have his own goals clearly in mind.

## INVESTMENT OBJECTIVES: LONG-TERM DEALS

If you're planning to invest in real estate for the long term, then it's probably best to form an LLC. I recommend an LLC for two reasons—asset protection and taxes. No business entity is bulletproof, but the LLC comes close because it addresses both the inside and outside liability issues that I briefly touched on earlier. Inside liability is fairly clear:

> Penny owns a country house that she rents out each summer to people looking to escape city life. Her attorney suggested that she put the house in an LLC for asset protection, which she did. Two years later a tenant's child is injured when he falls into an old well on the property. Penny never knew the well existed. The tenant attempt to sue Penny as the owner of the LLC, but soon discovered that the only recourse available is against the LLC.

A property owner is responsible for maintaining her land in a safe condition. In Penny's case, she is not the owner, and it is her LLC that owns the property and is responsible for maintenance. An attorney would like nothing better than to sue Penny individually, because the country house has very little equity and the wealthier the defendant, the greater the recourse. Fortunately for Penny, the law is on her side. The attorney can only look to the LLC for recovery, and in this case it is only the insurance and the minimal equity in the country house that is available. This form of protection is the primary reason why real estate investors utilize LLCs for their investments. The LLC forms a protective box around the asset, effectively cutting off the LLC members from any liabilities that arise inside of the box.

*To obtain more information on LLC operating agreements, go to www.andersonadvisors.com, register for a free Gold membership and search our article database for "Essential LLC Clauses."*

How? The protection comes from two places: state law and the LLC operating agreement that governs how the LLC is run and what protections it offers to its members. Most states are fairly uniform in their approach to inside protection. Liabilities that occur inside an LLC remain inside and will not attach to the owners of the LLC. Of course this is contingent upon there being a solid LLC operating agreement that has adequate protection and indemnification provisions for the members and managers. Unfortunately, it is not uncommon for me to review a client's operating agreement and to find two or three critical defects that if exposed in a lawsuit could spell disaster. Nevertheless, with the protection provided by state law and a good operating agreement, the LLC offers excellent protection from the liabilities associated with owning real estate.

Outside liability protection is just the opposite. Rather than looking to the assets of the LLC for recovery, a creditor is seeking a judgment against an LLC member because it is the member who caused the harm and not the LLC. Most people I meet completely miss this point because so much attention is given to protecting you from your real estate that very little thought is given to your personal actions or, for that matter, those of your children who could also jeopardize your investments. You, by your everyday actions, are probably the greatest threat to your assets.

> Nils, an avid real estate investor, is traveling in his new BMW 7-series sedan on Interstate 5. Confused by the electronics, his focus is on the stereo and not on the road! Because his attention is diverted, Nils does not see the car in front of him suddenly brake. Nils plows into the car, causing substantial damage to both vehicles and injuries to the occupants of the other vehicle.

If Nils owns his real estate investments in his personal name, he is at serious risk. Fortunately for Nils, his attorney recommended he place his investments in LLCs. How does the LLC help Nils? It has to do with state law and what the creditor of an LLC member can reach when he collects on his judgment.

Every state has, to some extent, given LLC members what the law refers to as charging order protections. Unlike the situation with inside liability where the creditor can only look to the assets of the LLC and not to the members individually for recovery, with outside liability the creditor is looking to recover against the member's assets. Your LLC membership interest, like the stock you own in a publicly traded company, is an asset. However, an important distinction, and possibly one that may spell the difference between ruin and success, is the availability of your LLC interest to a creditor. Unlike your stock in Microsoft, which can be seized to satisfy your creditor's judgment, an LLC membership interest is practically seizure-proof—because of the charging order!

## CHARGING ORDER PROTECTIONS

I use the term *charging order protections*, when in reality the charging order is a legal remedy provided to creditors who seek recovery against a member of an LLC. In Nils's situation, the injured parties will attempt to recover against all of Nils' assets until their judgment is paid in full. If Nils' major assets are his ownership interests in his LLCs, the injured parties will place a charging order on Nils' various LLC interests. A charging order does not do any of the following:

- Allow Nils' creditor to become a member in his LLC.
- Allow Nils' creditor to vote on LLC matters.
- Force Nils to sell his membership interests and distribute the proceeds to his creditor.
- Force Nils to liquidate his LLC and provide the proceeds to his creditor.
- Force Nils to distribute LLC profits.

You are probably wondering after reading this list why would anyone want a charging order. The answer is simple—Money. A charging order acts like a lien on the member's LLC interest. Nils' creditor will step into Nils' shoes whenever the LLC makes a distribution. This is how the creditor gets paid on his judgment, by placing what amounts to a lien on the member's LLC interest. As a result, all LLC distributions must be paid to Nils' creditor until the judgment is paid in full.

When I explain this point in my workshops, some people immediately question the benefits of using an LLC if all of the distributions will flow to a creditor. Sounds logical, but I must first remind these individuals about the inside protection benefits of the LLC and then proceed to challenge them to think outside of the box.

In Chapter 5, I discussed the basic structure of an LLC, and if you remember, I described how you will have complete control over your LLC as the LLC manager. Now, who do you think decides if the LLC will make any distributions—Give up? The manager! Now ask yourself this, what would you do in Nils' situation? Distribute LLC assets to enrich your creditor, or hold on to LLC assets? The answer is clear. As the manager, you undoubtedly decide to hold on to LLC assets for business reasons.

Many of the students I referred to above get the benefits of using an LLC without further explanation. You did not lose your assets in a lawsuit, and you still have control and ownership. What is not to like? Of course one or two holdouts who look at life as half-empty rather than half-full will tell me that if they can't make distributions, then they still fail to see the benefit of holding an asset locked away indefinitely in an LLC.

Again I must challenge these students to think outside the box. If someone asked you to manage their real estate (forget about real estate licensing issues for a moment), would you reply "absolutely and I will be happy to work for free"? Not likely. So if you are the manager of your LLC, will you perform this task for free, or does it sound reasonable that your LLCs should compensate you for your services? I will always come down on the side of getting paid. Who wants to work for free? Nils will confront his dilemma by changing the form of his income from distributions to a management fee. Nilse' creditor will most likely have some hard questions for his attorney as to why his judgment is not being paid.

One last point of consideration has to do with taxation. Many promoters of LLCs and LPs for asset protection falsely claim that a judgment creditor with a charging order will be responsible for the charged members' taxable interest in the entity—that your creditor will pay your taxes. This assumption is based on new Rule 77-137, but the authority of that ruling does not support the claim. However, do not tell anyone this important bit of information. The my-creditor-will-be-responsible-for-my-tax-liability mantra has become the stuff of urban legend, and I am happy enough to let the uninformed continue believing in these entities that not only protect assets but have the power to bite if you get too close.

## CHARGING ORDER PROBLEMS

The strategy I outlined for Nils works great when you own and control an LLC and it is filed in a favorable jurisdiction that recognizes the charging order as a creditor's sole remedy. Here are some examples of what could happen if you work with an attorney or asset protection specialist who does not understand the state-by-state differences in their approach to outside protection:

> Curt and Ernie form an LLC to operate a sporting goods store. Curt accumulates numerous gambling debts and doesn't have the money to pay them. His creditors take out a charging order against his interest in the company. While the creditors can lien Curt's membership interest in the company, they cannot attach the assets of the company (the sporting goods) since Curt, as a member, does not personally own the assets of his company.

> Rosemary owns three dress boutiques in California under an LLC she created over the Internet. When she accidentally starts a fire in her apartment, she is sued for negligence and found liable. The plaintiffs are awarded an unreasonable amount of money given the extent of their damages and in turn seek and receive a charging order against Rosemary's LLC membership interests. Rosemary, not wanting to make her creditors rich over a minor accident, discontinues all LLC distributions.

> Rosemary believes her business is safe but soon discovers this is not the case. Rosemary's creditors, not content receiving nothing under the charging order, are permitted to foreclose on her LLC interest. Rosemary loses her LLC and with it her business.

What happens next? In Curt's situation, the creditor will place a charging order on Curt's interest seeking all of the income and assets that will be distributed to Curt. However, Ernie and Curt can play it smart and simply stop making distributions of income. Now this strategy will definitely help Curt, but it will hurt Ernie because Ernie is accustomed to receiving distributions to cover his personal expenses.

Rosemary is not as lucky as Curt because she lost her interest. How could that happen? Rosemary thought the LLC would protect her from her personal creditors. Unfortunately for Rosemary, she did not consult an asset protection specialist about California law. Had she, Rosemary would have learned that California is one of several states that permit a creditor to foreclose on a member's LLC interest if the charging order is not sufficient as a remedy. So does the LLC truly protect your assets? The answer is that it depends. It depends on whom you use to create your plan. The asset protection specialist you choose must have a good working knowledge of each state's asset protection laws; otherwise, you could end up like Rosemary—not a very appealing proposition.

I assume you are probably wondering if there is a workable solution for Curt and Ernie wherein Ernie can continue to receive distributions without enriching Curt's creditors, or is it possible for Rosemary to protect her LLC despite California's relaxed asset protection laws. The answer is definitely YES, and I provide those solutions in Chapter 9.

## REAL ESTATE TAXATION AND LLCS

Asset protection is just one reason for holding long-term real estate in an LLC; the second is taxation. When you buy a property, you may not know exactly how long you plan to own it, but you should have some idea whether your investment is going to be long-term or short-term. The guidelines for dividing these two categories aren't set in stone, but, simply put, anything held for longer than one year is considered a long-term hold. That means your intent is to hold the property as an investment, and it actually *is* held for more than a year, rather than being just a quick turnaround.

A long-term hold provides some obvious advantages in terms of taxation. First, if you hold a property with the proper intent, for longer than one year, your capital gains taxes will change. Capital gains taxes are attributed to the profit or loss on the sale of an asset held for investment (such as real estate or stocks). The tax rate varies depending how long the property is held. In order to encourage buyers to hold property longer (and perhaps make improvements), the government offers reduced capital gains taxes the longer real estate is held. The reasons for this reduction in capital gains taxes are simple: You're not making profits the way you would if you were buying and selling the property, and there's always the depreciation factor of holding a property. If you keep your property for more than one year, you will reap significant reductions in this tax.

Capital gains rates can be complicated, but here's an example to show you how they can affect the average real estate investor.

> Ozzie decides to buy the home he grew up in as a child, but he is worried about the capital gains rates. He consults an attorney specializing in real estate deals. Initially, Ozzie had planned to spend 10 months fixing up the house and then sell

it to turn over a tidy profit within a year. His attorney advises him that the capital gains taxes on the sale of assets held for less than one year are pretty much the same as personal tax rates and that he possibly runs the risk of being classified as a dealer which could make him ineligible for capital gains taxes altogether (but rather liable for the higher regular personal income tax rate). His attorney tells him that if he holds on to the property for more than one year and lists it for rent instead of for sale when it is ready, his rate of taxation will only be 15% when he does sell. Ozzie sees the wisdom in this strategy and is willing to wait the extra few months to pay a reduced tax rate, and to collect rent on the property in the meantime. The difference in taxes owed to the government makes it all worthwhile.

You simply can't make any kind of investment in real estate and not think about your taxes. And how long you hold your property—as well as what you do with it—determines how much of your money the government gets. You are probably wondering: What do taxes have to do with LLCs? The answer is everything.

Ozzie did not consider real estate as a tax shelter when he bought his childhood home. To Ozzie, real estate investing is about making a profit—buy low, sell high. Ozzie missed a key feature of real estate ownership—depreciation. The government allows real estate owners to depreciate real estate held for investment. For many individuals, empires have been built around this concept because it allows an investor to earn income from rents and then offset the income against depreciation from the investment. Here is an example of how it works:

Chris purchases a modest six-unit property for $600,000 in an LLC that he owns and controls. After calculating his operating costs and debt service, Chris is pleasantly surprised that he will collect $10,000 in positive annual cash flow. Chris decides to play it smart and put aside $3,000 for his estimated income taxes, but when he speaks to his CPA he is amazed to learn that his investment can be depreciated over 39 years. His CPA calculates Chris' annual depreciation to be $12,000 and informs Chris not to worry about taxes on his rental income. Chris won't owe a dime.

Amazing, just by owning real estate Chris will not owe any tax on his yearly profit, and it gets even better. Because Chris's depreciation exceeds his rental income by $2,000, Chris has a loss that he can use against rental income from other properties or against the salary he earns as a local fireman. Now don't get carried away and think that Chris is losing money, because he is not. The loss is on paper.

Depreciation is considered a paper loss because you are not losing actual cash in your account. The loss will appear on your tax return, but you keep the money. Does this sound too good to be true? It's not, so long as you understand that you will recoup the loss when you sell the property. Although an in-depth explanation of real estate taxation is beyond the purpose of this book, you can find additional information at www.andersonadvisors.com. Sign up as a member, then search for articles on real estate taxation. You will definitely get your fill of tax information.

The $2,000 excess loss Chris offsets against his fireman's salary is available provided he owns the building in his own name (not an option) or in an LLC. A corporation or limited partnership are not options because these entities will trap excess losses and not allow the owners to reap a personal benefit on their individual income tax returns. The reason for this is simple. To be eligible for excess depreciation capture on a personal income tax return, the investor must own the property (directly or indirectly through an entity) and exercise control over the property. In a limited partnership, you satisfy the ownership test but not the control test. Remember from our discussion in Chapter 5 that control rests with the general partner but not with the limited partners. In a corporation, the losses will not flow through, and thus become trapped. In contrast, the flow-through characteristics of an LLC coupled with the members' ability to exercise control without sacrificing their liability protection makes the LLC the ideal entity for holding real estate for the long-term.

## ONE LLC FOR EACH PROPERTY

One LLC per property has many advantages, and it's actually the core of good asset protection for real estate investors. Why?

> Regan buys a bookstore and plans to renovate and make changes. She creates an LLC to own the bookstore as well as her personal residence. Unfortunately, a customer in her new bookstore slips on the imported mosaic tiles, sues Regan's LLC, and wins a huge settlement in court. The bookstore doesn't have enough profits to cover the damages, and much to Regan's horror the court orders her to pay out of her pocket, or out of the sale of her home. Her mistake? Using an LLC to cover multiple properties can have a domino effect—if one property is under suit, the others can be too.

Clearly, if Regan had created one LLC just for her bookstore, then a court must work through numerous formalities to pierce the LLC and reach her personal assets. Instead, she made it easy for them by throwing all her assets into one big LLC, and she now risks losing not just her bookstore but her house as well. A better approach would have been the one taken by Merv:

> Merv has four properties with roughly $35,000 in equity per property. Merv consults an attorney who recommends Merv create four LLCs; one for each of his properties. Several months later one of his tenants is hosting a 40th birthday party for his wife. Several of the tenant's guests are severely injured when the 2nd story deck they were standing on collapsed due to rotten timbers. Fortunately for Merv, this property was in an LLC without any other assets. Merv's total exposure is $35,000, his total equity in the property. Merv learned that when it comes to protecting real estate investments, placing one property per LLC is a sound strategy.

For some investors, this can be an expensive proposition if their properties are located in a state with high taxes or entity fees. An alternative to the one property per LLC is the equity approach to funding. Under the equity approach, the investor determines his risk tolerance level target for each LLC—say, $250,000. In this way, a careful investor can safeguard his properties by dividing them among a given number of LLCs.

*When creating a LLC keep in mind that Manager-Managed is preferrable to Member-Managed and Disregarded tax status is preferrable to Partnership tax status in most situations.*

A second consideration worthy of mention when deciding how many LLCs to create is how rich your CPA will become from all the work you will be providing him. Students at my workshops who see the value in the protection but are discouraged by the perceived annual maintenance costs raise this point time and time again. It is a great point and I agree with them, but there is an answer—use single-member LLCs. As I briefly mentioned in Chapter 5, a truly unique entity is the disregarded LLC.

A disregarded LLC is not a different form of business entity, rather it is an LLC that has a single member and has elected to be disregarded for federal taxes. A disregarded LLC is not required to file a separate tax return for profits and losses if the owner's federal tax return reflects those changes. I am sure you can see how, from an annual cost perspective, this can amount to several thousand dollars if multiple LLCs are involved. In Merv's situation, if all four of his LLCs were disregarded, he would only file his personal income tax return each year. His CPA would not incur any additional work as a result of Merv's structuring.

## PARTNERING WITH OTHERS ON REAL ESTATE INVESTMENTS

In many cases, it may be advantageous to partner with someone when you're investing in real estate. It may be tempting to immediately go into an LLC because it seems like the most obvious plan for two people to go into business together. However, this plan is very dangerous because investors need to think a step ahead before joining together to form an LLC. Here's an example:

> Randy and Mitch decide to invest in a rundown 12-unit apartment building in a trendy neighborhood. Their plan is to renovate the building through a condo conversion of the property. Aware of the liabilities associated with real estate investing, Randy and Mitch consult a local attorney, who recommends they form an LLC for their project. As the project nears its completion, Mitch is served with a lawsuit stemming

from an auto accident he was involved in prior to meeting Randy. Mitch asks Randy not to distribute any profits from the LLC until he resolves the lawsuit, but Randy is need of money to pay off a loan that is maturing within the month.

Do you notice a problem with this strategy? In reality, unless the partners are married or related, it's almost always best to form individual LLCs that protect your interest in the property without necessarily tying you down to your partner or his liabilities. In the case of Randy and Mitch, each of them is forced to deal with the other person's liabilities. A preferable method would be one wherein Randy and Mitch create separate LLCs to own the project LLC. This way each of them can control the timing of their own distributions and depending where they set up their LLCs, their involvement could be masked by a nominee manager.

## WHERE SHOULD YOUR LLC BE ORGANIZED?

Where you create your LLC is also important. In most cases, people choose to file their operating agreement for their LLC in the state where the LLC is most likely to operate. Unlike corporations, LLCs aren't automatically filed in the state where the LLC does business, though in instances where an LLC is created to manage, purchase, and sell real estate, it's best to have the LLC set up in the state where the property is located. Why? It's a matter of practicality, and in cases of liability, it may be the simplest way to deal with real estate. Many landlords and building sellers are reluctant to deal with sellers who are based in other states and who may be following different procedures and rules. When it comes to real estate, it's almost always beneficial to file in the state where the property is located.

There *are* those investors who decide to file in a state other than where the property is held. In most cases, the state they choose to file in is either Delaware or Nevada. Historically, Delaware's favorable corporate laws have made it a favorite location to base corporate entities of all sizes, simply because it offers more protection for the owner and members. For example, Delaware is one of only a handful of states that allow a series LLC. In recent years, Nevada's regulations have opened up for real estate investors, encouraging them to form their business entities in Nevada even if their properties are located elsewhere. I generally advise that all entities that deal with real property be formed in the state where the property is located. Even if you form the LLC in Nevada, you will still have to register or file with the state where the real property you're trying to buy is located in order to do business in that state. Depending on the state where your property is located, this may not provide added protection but could possibly add to the cost.

For the most part, we have discussed long-term deals—property owned for at least a year, preferably more, without the goal of selling to make a quick profit. When you are engaged in short-term deals and flipping property to make more there are other ramifications, not the least of which is that you might be considered a real estate dealer. As professional as this title sounds, you do not want to be considered a real estate dealer, or someone who makes his living buying and selling property. Dealer status is determined by many factors, some of which are open issues in courts today. I'll discuss dealer status in the next section, but for now simply know that you do not want to appear as a real estate dealer.

# Short-Term Investing—  *Quick Turns, Wholesaling, and Other Strategies*

There is a question that I am asked more than any other, and it is: "Am I or will I be a real estate dealer?" Why this question? Because the Internet and infomercials have created a situation where there is a subtraction of good real estate tax information by the addition of real estate investment gurus. Each self-proclaimed investment expert attempts to establish credibility by offering advice on a subject matter they know little about. It is simple to read a bit of information and believe you understand it, but like most tax or asset protection issues the devil is in the details.

> Tracy's accountant suggests that she start buying and selling small rental properties downtown to make some extra cash and maximize some of the profits from her existing properties. He gives her a quick overview of dealer status, and Tracy decides that she's only going to sell four properties this year. She recalls hearing that the IRS considers you a dealer if you flip five or more properties. Unfortunately, she should have checked her facts. When the IRS looks at Tracy's real estate deals, it analyzes

> *To obtain more information on dealer status go to www.andersonadvisors.com, register for a free Gold membership and sign up for my free email newsletter. Each month you will receive up-to-date tax information that will help you keep more of what you earn.*

her intent. In the end, the IRS considered Tracy a dealer for all property sales even though one property was held for more than two years. Tracy lost all the benefits given investors.

Clearly, you want to avoid dealer status because your dealer type actions can taint *all* of your property sales. There are no easy guidelines, and a good asset protection specialist who knows both the tax code and the tax laws will be able to give you a clear idea of what you're heading for when you decide to buy and sell real estate for a profit. Your specialist can also give you some ideas on how to avoid dealer status. Below are two examples of investors who may or may not be dealers. Can you guess which one the IRS considered to be an ordinary investor, and who was considered to be a real estate dealer?

> William owns an apartment building in the city, a country house, a beachfront condo, and a cabin in the woods, all in the same state, all under renovation, all of which he's owned for a few years. He has no immediate plans to sell the properties until they're completely finished. He may sell them eventually, but when his stock portfolio takes a sudden dive he realizes that he must sell some of his properties in order to stay solvent. William puts a real estate agent in charge of the sale and speeds up the renovation, and, before the end of the year, he has sold everything but the apartments in the city, which he continues to seek tenants for.

> Xavier buys a large warehouse and immediately divides it up into smaller condos. He has a small office space near the property to deal with the renovations and the sales, and he is closely involved in the day-to-day activities of the property, including actively soliciting buyers for the condos with phone calls and less than a year after Xavier bought the property, all nine condos in the warehouse space were sold or rented.

So, who is the dealer? Xavier is pretty upset to find out that after looking at all the factors, the IRS considers him a dealer. Some of the factors the IRS looked at included the fact that Xavier purchased office space to deal with the sale property. He also subdivided the property to increase sales, and he closely supervised the real estate agent and day-to-day construction workers. Xavier spent a significant portion of time and money managing and renovating the property, all of which tells the IRS that he always had the intent to sell. Unlike William, Xavier did not sell because he was suddenly faced with financial hardship; Xavier was always involved in upgrading, improving, and selling the property. Also unlike William, Xavier owned the warehouse only briefly before all the sales went through, while William owned his property for some time before he decided to sell. While both worked at improving their properties, Xavier's improvements substantially increased the possibility of sale; he created the condos. William, on the other hand, was involved in more conventional renovations that were not necessarily motivated by wanting to sell the properties. These are just some of the factors that the IRS looks at when determining dealer status. The difference can mean tens of thousands of dollars staying in your pocket rather than going to the IRS.

Developers, in addition to the possible significant liability exposure, are also at risk of being classified as a dealer. A property developer will typically find a large parcel of land to break up into smaller lots to either sell after utilities are installed or after homes are constructed. This form of investing, outside of the liabilities for the developer, can significantly increase your tax liability if not properly structured through a corporation. Consider the following example.

> Anticipating an increased demand for custom homes on 5-acre tracts, Cory purchases 50 acres in Ellensburg, Washington, from a retired farmer. After waiting two years, Cory decides the market is right for development. Cory works with his local real estate attorney to divide the land into separate lots and begin installation of utilities. Within one year, Cory has constructed and sold four homes for a $450,000 profit. Cory is ecstatic about his development until he meets with his accountant to prepare his taxes; Cory is stunned to discover that all of his profits will be taxed as ordinary income. Cory thought by holding the property for more than a year before selling his first lot he could benefit from long-term capital gains treatment. Cory is considered a dealer.

Cory's situation is common among real estate investors who rely on their local attorney who lacks the correct asset protection and tax knowledge necessary in creating a quality plan. Many attorneys will only do what is asked of them and not recommend alternative strategies. The reason for this stems from how attorneys are trained. In law school, future attorneys are taught to prepare client engagement letters outlining the scope of services to be provided. If a client walks into an attorney's office and asks him for assistance in subdividing land, the engagement letter will limit the scope of the attorney's services to the subdivision. Attorneys do not like to work outside the scope of the agreement for fear of liability. In Cory's situation, he did not ask his attorney how to structure his subdivision from an asset protection or tax standpoint, so no advice was offered.

If Cory had consulted my office, I would have explained that prior to subdividing his property he needed to set up a corporation for asset protection and tax planning. The corporation will protect Cory individually from injured workers or the multitude of other liabilities common with development projects, in addition to alleviating some of his taxes.

From a tax standpoint, the corporation is great for property developers because it isolates development activity from investment activity. Cory held the property for more than one year prior to beginning his development. If Cory sold the 50 acres outright, his tax rate would be 15%, but in developing the property Cory increased his tax rate to 35%. Cory's mistake was in not selling the undivided land to his corporation. Such a sale would qualify for long-term capital gain tax treatment, while the subsequent development income is taxed at regular corporate rates. Cory could effectively split his taxes between development activity and investment activity thereby saving Cory several hundred thousand dollars in taxes.

William, Xavier, Tracy, and Cory all made the same mistake in their investing—none of them received proper guidance on how to avoid dealer status. The good news is that it's relatively simple to make sure you do not qualify as a dealer, as long as you know the factors that go into being classified as a dealer and then plan accordingly.

## KNOW WHAT MAKES A DEALER, AND PLAN ACCORDINGLY

A dealer is someone who buys and sells property to make money, and uses it as one of his primary sources of income. There are a lot of factors that go into whether you are considered a real estate dealer. Some factors are easy to spot—how many properties did you buy and sell in the last year? Do you have an office where you run your real estate business? Did you attend educational workshops on buying and flipping, or turning around, real estate? Is your income from the properties simply the rent that your tenants pay you, or are you generating most of your income from remodeling and reselling property? Investors who make their living renovating property to flip, wholesale, or scout are also considered dealers. Many land developers, pre-construction speculators, and builders are also considered dealers, depending on the circumstances.

*Deciding if you are a dealer comes down to intent. If your intent is to buy and sell real estate, then the IRS may consider you a dealer so keep good business records as to your intent with respect to your real estate.*

So who determines whether you're a dealer? Bad news—the IRS does. The question is your intent when purchasing and selling the property. You may think that no court can accurately guess your intent, particularly if you play things close to the vest, but a court simply looks at your actions, your documents, your deals, and then makes a determination of your intent. The ultimate question is: Are you holding the property as an investment, or as a sale waiting to happen?

Being considered a dealer can be a very bad thing, simply because you give up many of the tax benefits of a real estate investor. As a dealer you end up paying a lot more money to the IRS. The most obvious drawback is the difference in your capital gains taxes. An ordinary investor who is not considered a dealer will pay only 15% in capital gains taxes when he sells property held for more than one year. A dealer could well pay as much as 35%. That could mean thousands of dollars to the IRS that should be in your pocket. Additionally, a dealer cannot use the installment method to calculate tax payments—something that is normally available to every real estate investor. Instead of paying taxes only as you collect income from the property, you must pay taxes on the whole profit immediately—whether or not the money is actually in the bank. You lose §1031 exchange treatments for properties you sell, since the property is considered inventory, and will lose all the depreciation that would normally be listed on your tax return. Even worse, a dealer may be subject to self-employment tax on all of his real estate transactions.

This can be bad news for those investors who would like to buy and sell a certain number of properties per year. Not knowing how the IRS makes this determination can cause some serious problems for you. Clearly, dealer status is something that the average real estate investor wants to avoid. The question, of course, is how.

## AVOIDING DEALER STATUS

If you're planning on doing some short-term real estate deals, dealer status is something that you need to be very worried about. Dealer status is not a test the IRS likes to apply on a deal-by-deal basis, although an argument can be made for such an application. The IRS will most likely look at your overall real estate related activity and make a determination as to your general intent. Consider the following example of Vinny who sells vehicles instead of real estate:

Vinny owns a BMW dealership in his own name. In addition to selling BMWs, Vinny enjoys acquiring vintage BMWs for his private collection. With the increasing popularity of classic vehicles, Vinny's collection has appreciated significantly over the past five years. Unfortunately for Vinny, the economy in his local area experiences a significant downturn when the local high-flying technology company decides to move its office to a warmer location. Vinny, in need of some quick cash, must part with several of the vehicles in his personal collection. Vinny reports the income from these sales as long-term capital gains because he held these vehicles for investment and not in the ordinary course of his business. However, the IRS disagreed with Vinny and made him re-characterize the sales as ordinary income. The IRS treated Vinny's collectable vehicles as inventory.

In Vinny's situation he thought he could be a collector and a dealer, but the IRS thought otherwise. Real estate is the investor's vehicle. Trying to flip properties under your own name, as a sole proprietorship, or even as an LLC, will not be much help to you in terms of conducting business as an investor rather than as a dealer. However, you can avoid dealer status when you're investing in the short-term.

Perhaps the most useful tool for avoiding dealer status is doing business as a corporation. A corporation is great at insulating its owners from the corporation's business activity. All of your short-term property deals get reported under the corporation's employer identification number and not your social security number. You may be wondering why not an LLC? The answer is simple: From a tax perspective, the LLC does not offer the same protection because it allows dealer activity to filter down on to the LLC member's tax return. The key to avoiding dealer status is in keeping dealer-type activity locked away in a corporation. With a corporation you not only avoid liability from lawsuits, but you also decrease the tax liabilities that often come from flipping properties.

At this point you probably have a good understanding of the different forms of investing that can infringe on dealer territory. So you might be asking if you should treat this form of real estate investing the same as long-term holds, i.e. set up multiple corporations for each form of investing? The unequivocal answer is No—unless of course you have a strong desire to keep your CPA driving his 7 series BMW for the next 20 years.

Multiple corporations equal multiple tax returns, multiple bank accounts, multiple corporate recordkeeping, and the list goes on and on. Unlike the relaxed structure of an LLC, a corporation requires a lot of annual work to maintain its status. If you would rather focus on the business in lieu of being in business, then stock up on corporations, because you will have a full plate keeping up with the formalities. Remember, corporations are not for holding assets for any length of time so that your risk exposure from different business ventures in one entity is quite low from a loss perspective. In essence, corporations should be used sparingly and should own next to nothing.

Ideally, your corporation should not be holding much in the way of assets except a current rehab or two. If the corporation has few assets, then little is at risk in the event of a lawsuit. Contrast this with LLCs that hold real estate for an extended length of time for investment. In the latter situation you should be keenly aware of how many LLCs are needed to minimize your risk exposure; thus, several are often recommended. Unlike holding real estate for the long-term, the number of corporations required for handling multiple rehabs is one. However, you have learned from reading this book that isolation of liability is a key component of asset protection. How then can people protect themselves when their corporation is involved in multiple projects? By taking a page from my chapter on long-term holding and applying the same principles with one slight deviation—Your corporation will be the owner of its own LLCs. Consider the example of Rod who is likely to have several rehabs in his corporation at any given time.

> Rod caught the property rehab bug from witnessing all of the bank-owned REO properties recently made available in his local area. Rod, flush with cash raised from friends and family, saw the real estate downturn as an opportunity to make his fortune. Rod set up a corporation and began acquiring several properties under his corporate name. Within two months Rod's corporation owned five properties, and he was extremely busy rehabbing two of them. Rod's hard work paid off, and within four months Rod sold his first rehab for a tidy profit of $75,000. Rod was excited with his payday and eagerly worked on his remaining properties.
>
> Unfortunately for Rod the contractor who installed the gas stove in the house Rod recently sold used the wrong type of pipe. As a result of the faulty pipe, the house caught fire and injured the new homeowners. Needless to say, they sued Rod's corporation. As a result of the lawsuit, all of Rod's rehab work ground to a halt and the plaintiff's attorney sought to recover against the corporation's assets—the remaining four houses. Rod was out of business, and he was left to answer to all his friends and family who had invested in his business.

Rod could have solved his liability problem by establishing a minimum of two LLCS to hold his rehab properties. The LLCs in turn would be owned and managed by Rod's corporation. By employing the same diversification principles we use for rental real estate, Rod could limit his overall risk exposure to the number of properties held per LLC. When Rod is purchasing properties he will buy them in the name of his LLCs, taking care to balance his overall equity among the two entities. Should something occur with a particular property resulting in liability, Rod's overall risk exposure is limited to the LLC that own(s)(ed) the property. The corporation and the other LLC can continue work unaffected by this problem. If you are having trouble seeing my point, review the previous chapter on LLCs, and it should become clearer.

One last point on this strategy before we discuss the benefits of Nevada corporations for the real estate investor; I will encourage my clients who adopt this structure to develop no more than ten to fifteen properties in an LLC and then to dissolve it and create a new one. By dissolving the LLC, you will send a message to any would-be plaintiffs that the business they were planning to sue is no longer operating and is in fact dissolved. What type of message does this send—dollar signs or debt? I am not sure even the hungriest of attorneys is willing to bring a claim against a dead and possibly debt-laden entity.

## WHERE SHOULD YOU INCORPORATE?

When I sit down with a prospective client, the first question I am asked is: "Where should I incorporate?" Not "Do you think I need a corporation given my business plan?" Most people I meet with typically come to the conclusion on their own that they need a corporation for their real estate investing. When I ask how they see a corporation benefiting them, I typically receive the following responses:

- I plan to buy and sell property and I want to avoid dealer status.
- I would like to manage my rental properties with a formal structure so my tenants do not know I own the property.
- I like the tax breaks a corporation provides for my business and I am tired of paying too much in tax.
- I plan to strip the equity in my properties with a friendly lien to keep potential creditors at bay. And,
- In your talk you made it sound as if everyone should have a corporation so here I am.

With the exception of the last comment, each of the reasons given for incorporating makes sense. The comments show a genuine understanding of the benefits a corporation offers. So the next point of consideration becomes where you incorporate.

Real estate investors must always register their corporation in each state where business activity is conducted. Business activity consists of buying and selling, rehabbing, wholesaling, managing, or just about anything that involves dealing with the public. So do you just pick a state where you plan to conduct business and incorporate? Not quite, because knowing the ins and outs of each state when it comes to asset protection and taxation could potentially save your bottom line or your "assets" in the event of a lawsuit.

Here's an example:

> After attending a few workshops on real estate investing, Gene was ready to begin investing in bank-owned properties. Gene remembered that one of the workshop speakers stated that he should set up a corporation for his investing. Heeding the advice of the speaker, Gene incorporated himself in his home state of California. After incorporating, Gene began acquiring

properties in California, Arizona, and Florida. By December Gene had bought and sold more than 12 properties through his corporation, generating a tidy profit for his business. When Gene consulted with his CPA on some yearend planning strategies, he was dismayed to learn that all of the income his corporation generated from selling properties in Arizona and Florida was taxable in California. Gene couldn't understand why California could tax income generated from business generated outside of California. His CPA explained that California imposes a tax on all business income regardless of its source.

Gene's story is not uncommon among many investors who rush to incorporate without first seeking the advice of an asset protection attorney who understands the issues of taxation and business formation across state lines. Gene would have been well-served to incorporate in Nevada rather than registering to conduct business in California, Arizona, and Florida. In exchange for incurring an additional incorporation fee in Nevada, Gene could apportion his income to the states where it was earned, thus avoiding California taxing every nickel regardless of its source.

When it comes to choosing where to incorporate your business, think about where you plan to invest today and in the future. If you plan to invest outside of the state in which you live, then you should definitely consider incorporating in a business-friendly state and then registering your corporation in every state in which you plan to conduct business. In addition to where you will actually conduct your business, other less obvious factors should be considered when deciding where to incorporate.

In recent years, Nevada has emerged as a state that is very sympathetic to real estate investors. While Delaware has traditionally been the state most favorable to incorporation, Delaware companies still have to give public reports and are likely to be taxed. Nevada, on the other hand, is a business haven because of the protection it gives corporate entities, and the difficulty of piercing those corporate entities to get to the owners, shareholders, or members.

Creating a corporate entity in Nevada has never been easier, but the state law does require that you have a Nevada-based agent or representative. You may be wondering why you would incorporate in Nevada when you have no intention of doing business there. Anonymity is a key factor: When an attorney who's considering a lawsuit against you does a search, he won't find anything under your name if you've incorporated in Nevada. Nevada requires virtually no public reporting, no residency requirements of shareholders/members, and makes it extraordinarily easy to set up a corporation. You may buy and sell property with your Nevada corporation, even though it is taxed and treated as an entirely separate entity from you.

There are hundreds of offers on the Internet to get you incorporated in Nevada, using special forms, kits, and advice from "bulletproof" investors. The reality is that a Nevada corporation is easy to set up, but you shouldn't be doing it with a kit. A kit is simply a bunch of generic forms that set up the structure of your corporation: shareholder's meetings, articles of organization, etc. You could easily use the kit to keep your corporation running, but if you don't understand which forms are more important than others, or how to personalize the forms to your individual situation, the kit—and any advice you get online—is useless. Investment gurus who try to pitch you a Nevada corporation without looking carefully at your business and how you run it are simply trying to make a buck. Incorporating, even in a state as corporation-friendly as Nevada, is not something you do blindly; only an asset protection specialist can look at your investments and portfolio from the right perspective and set up a system of corporate entities to protect your savings.

A Nevada corporation can also be very useful in hiding the equity in the property. How? Well, remember equity stripping? Your Nevada corporation could file a friendly lien against your property, which becomes encumbered by that lien. Remember, properties with liens are much less attractive to lawyers; it's too much trouble to sell a house that has multiple liens against it. In this case, you're essentially putting a lien upon yourself, but because the Nevada corporation is completely anonymous it doesn't look like it's you. In most cases, neither the IRS nor your creditors can pierce the veil of a Nevada corporation to get at you, which means that as long as no one knows that you've put a friendly lien on yourself, you have just hidden the value of your real estate and made it less attractive to potential predators.

Here's an example:

> Yolanda owns two summer homes, one in Maine and one in Florida. She decides to incorporate in Nevada, and on the advice of an asset protection specialist, files liens on both her summer homes. When sued by a disgruntled nanny six months later, Yolanda knows that her homes are protected since they both have numerous liens filed upon them by a Nevada corporation. The nanny and her attorney do a search of Yolanda's assets and find out that not only are her summer homes mortgaged and encumbered, but they can't find out more about the Nevada corporation that is holding the liens against the properties. Without a name or a clear path to Yolanda's assets, the nanny's attorney convinces her to drop the suit. If Yolanda had incorporated in Delaware instead of Nevada, the attorney might have realized that Yolanda was

simply engaging in some clever equity stripping, and that she was simply putting friendly liens on herself. But because of Nevada's strict anonymity policy and history of not allowing piercing of the corporate veil, Yolanda has managed to safeguard both her summer homes.

It should be fairly obvious that when it comes to deciding where to incorporate your business, it is very important to know what you're doing. If you simply buy a kit or follow some online instructions, you're doing your assets a disservice. There are many factors that go into deciding where to incorporate, and my examples have only gone over a few. Your asset protection specialist, if he understands both the legal and tax consequences of corporate entities, should be able to protect your assets and keep you from making mistakes.

# IRAs and Real Estate

One area of investing that always generates interest and many questions among my workshop attendees is IRAs and real estate. In the mid-2000s, real estate investors saw their IRAs as an untapped source of cash that could be put to use in real estate. Around this same time, many questionable real estate investment gurus began springing up all over the country touting the latest and greatest investing strategies. For thousands of dollars anyone could learn the secrets of real estate investing and become a millionaire. As investors acquired real estate, they found out relatively quickly that banks would only provide a limited number of loans, so absent a creative financing techniques, some investors were locked out of the market without an alternative source of funding. It didn't take long for investors in need of further investment capital to consider the untapped wealth they held in their IRAs as a possible alternative source. Here is an example of an investor looking to use their IRA for real estate investing:

> After attending a seminar on real estate investing, Randy hit the ground running and within a year had acquired twelve properties with the help of his local bank. Randy, deciding on a career as a real estate investor, left his job and devoted all his

time to real estate. When Randy took his latest deal to his bank, he was dismayed to learn that the bank would not loan him any more money. Randy did not know where to turn. He knew about hard money loans, but the terms of these loans would considerably diminish the rate of return on his investments. Fortunately for Randy, he had elected to roll over his 401k from his prior employer into an IRA. When Randy called his broker and told him of his plans to use the IRA funds for real estate investing, the broker told Randy it was not permitted. Out of options, Randy gave up on investing and found a job with a new employer.

Randy's experience is not uncommon. Many investors have told me that when they talk to their IRA custodian they are told the investment is not permitted. I explain that the problem is their custodian and not the investment. IRAs are permitted to invest in real estate, but most IRA custodians do not allow these investments. Why? The answer is money. IRA custodians make money from holding and investing your money. If you are allowed to direct your investments away from your custodian, the custodian loses control and the ability to generate commissions from money off your investments.

Section 408 of the Internal Revenue Code allows individuals (not corporate entities) to hold property under an IRA, using an IRA custodian (who is not the account holder). An IRA custodian holds legal title to the property and will help you set this up for a fee, but if he does not make an effort to collect rent and pay the bills, then you will have to take care of those matters yourself. Most IRA custodians charge a fee for their services, and there's a great deal of paperwork, so it's important to get someone who knows what he's doing and knows how to maximize your profit and minimize your liability. These custodians permit people to establish what is commonly referred to as a self-directed IRA.

A self-directed IRA is not a specific type of IRA like a ROTH IRA or a Simple IRA. A self-directed IRA describes the power the IRA beneficiary holds over his IRA funds. With a self-directed IRA, the beneficiary is the one in control of his investment choices because he is not limited by his IRA custodian. In a truly self-directed IRA the custodian will make investments upon the direction of the IRA owner, provided of course the investment choices do not fall within the IRA prohibited transaction rules. The key is finding a reputable custodian who is knowledgeable about IRA investing. A simple search on the Internet will produce hundreds of hits for companies that promote and/or offer self-directed IRAs. In my experience, the vast majority of these companies are comprised of salesmen who have little knowledge of the tax code and its restrictions on IRA investments. Like a flip side of the typical IRA custodian who does not want you to direct your own investments, these questionable companies are more than willing to give you unfettered control in exchange for a fee. The problem every investor faces with a self-directed IRA is knowing the IRA's limitation.

> Brad establishes a ROTH IRA with IRA Maximizer, Inc., a company he found on the Internet that specializes in creating self-directed IRAs. Brad was pleased with the initial help he received from IRA Maximizer in assisting him roll over his existing ROTH IRA with E-Trade to his new self directed IRA with IRA Maximizer. When Brad found a small apartment building he wished to purchase with his ROTH IRA, his new custodian was extremely helpful in assisting Brad with his purchase. Everything ran smoothly until the following year when Brad received his property tax bill for $8,000 and his ROTH account only had $500. Brad calls his custodian about the dilemma, and Brad is told the real estate company he owns

with his son could loan his ROTH IRA the money needed to cover the tax provided the company properly documented the transaction. Brad loaned his ROTH IRA the money to cover his taxes and carefully documented the loan per the custodian's instructions.

Joe has a small traditional IRA with a company that permits him to direct the investments. Joe would like to purchase property inside of his IRA, but he does not have enough funds to cover anything other than a fixer-upper. Joe relents and purchases a house in his IRA that he plans to renovate, and then lease. Joe asks his IRA custodian how he should go about renovating the property, and Joe is told not to use any of his personal funds for the renovation. All monies must come from Joe's IRA. Joe heeds his custodian's advice and begins work immediately, paying for all the materials from his IRA. After 3 months of hard work, Joe has his investment property ready to rent.

Jill does not want to be a landlord, but she is intrigued by the quick returns to be made from buying or optioning property from distressed sellers. Jill is excited about the prospect but she has poor credit and minimal savings. After attending a seminar on real estate investing, Jill learns how to find undervalued properties and sell them for a quick profit on a tax-free basis inside of her ROTH IRA. Jill is intrigued, and after a quick consult with her ROTH IRA custodian she begins buying and selling properties on a monthly basis. Eighteen deals later, Jill has generated a 200% return in her ROTH IRA and is on her way to financial independence.

Did any of these people engage in a prohibited transaction? You may be surprised to learn that all of them did in one form or another. Under Section 4975 of the Internal Revenue Code, any transaction between an IRA and a "disqualified person" is considered a prohibited transaction. A "disqualified person" is defined as:

- The IRA owner
- The IRA owner's spouse, parents, grandparents, children, and grandchildren
- The spouses of the IRA owner's children or grandchildren
- The IRA owner's custodian or trustee
- An entity or trust more than 50% owned by any combination of the foregoing
- A 10% owner, officer, director, or highly compensated employee of such entity
- Any person providing services to the IRA

If your IRA is found to have engaged in a prohibited transaction with any of the disqualified persons above, it ceases to be an IRA, resulting in a taxable distribution of the IRA assets, a 10% early distribution penalty if you are under age 59½, and a 15% excise tax on the amount involved. So what is a prohibited transaction? This is where it gets tricky and why you need to work with a competent professional because the stakes are too high when dealing with your retirement funds. Here is how Section 4975 defines a prohibited transaction:

- Sale, exchange, or leasing of property between an IRA and a disqualified person
- Lending of money or other extension of credit to a disqualified person
- Furnishing of goods, services, or facilities to a disqualified person
- Transfer to or use of IRA income or assets to a disqualified person

- Indirect use of IRA income or assets for the benefit of a disqualified person
- Receipt of any consideration by a disqualified person from his own account or from any party dealing with the IRA in connection with a transaction involving plan assets

In Brad's situation, he engaged in a prohibited transaction when the corporation he owned with his son loaned his ROTH IRA $8,000 to cover its property taxes. Had Brad worked with a reputable IRA custodian, he would have been advised against loaning money to his ROTH IRA, because Brad's corporation is considered a disqualified person. Remember, an IRA owner or disqualified person cannot loan assets to his IRA for its use. Brad could have easily avoided engaging in a prohibited transaction and covered his property taxes with some creative thinking by consulting an advisor with a thorough understanding of the prohibited transaction rules. If Brad had called my firm, we might have recommend Brad's ROTH IRA borrow from an unrelated third party, pay the property taxes late, make a partial ROTH conversion from any other traditional IRA he owns, or consider making an intentional excess contribution to his ROTH IRA and correct it by April 15 of the following year.

*I have met several students at my workshops who have used their IRA in an inappropriate manner when it comes to real estate investing. One person was told she could receive a commission when she sold real estate through her IRA. Each and every time the she received advice from a company specializing in self directed IRAs.*

Joe probably assumed that by having his IRA pay for all the materials, he was operating in the clear when he rehabbed his property. Unfortunately for Joe, he only received half of the story from his IRA custodian. Joe performed the rehab work himself. As a disqualified person, Joe is not allowed to furnish services to his IRA. The worked performed by Joe is considered an impressible contribution of personal services by a disqualified person. Joe should have hired a contractor to handle the rehab work.

Jill's situation appears to fall outside of Section 4975 prohibitions. Jill's actions on the surface appear to be no different than those of a person who buys and sells stock inside of his IRA. In Jill's case, her stock was houses that she purchased low and sold high for a quick profit with the help of her IRA custodian. What Jill didn't realize is that Section 4975 is not the only code section she must be aware of when investing in an IRA. Jill had hoped to buy and sell real estate tax-free inside of her ROTH IRA; however, Jill's activities will most likely rise to the level of an active trade or business.

Most investors I meet have no idea that real estate investing can be considered an active trade or business. In Chapter 7, I discussed short-term investing and the risk of dealer status. Dealer status occurs when real estate investment activity rises to a level that is no longer considered passive in nature. In other words, is Jill's IRA merely holding real estate for rent or appreciation, or is her intent to buy and to sell for short-term market gain? Eighteen deals in one year appear on the surface to be active and not passive in nature. When an IRA engages in an active trade or business, Section 511 of the Internal Revenue Code will impose a tax on all income generated inside of the IRA. So much for Jill's desire for tax-free investing.

All three of these examples should illustrate the minefield you or your custodian must navigate to keep your IRA out of trouble. Real estate investing inside of an IRA is permissible and does not have to invalidate your IRA, but it should be approached cautiously. There is no point in investing in real estate through your IRA if it creates more problems for you than solutions.

## STEPS TO ACQUIRING REAL ESTATE IN AN IRA:

1. Locate property to purchase.

2. Roll over enough money to complete the transaction into a self-directed IRA. Note: Each real estate transaction should be conducted through a separate IRA. That way, if a prohibited transaction occurs, only the funds in one IRA will be tainted and not those in your other IRAs.

3. IRA owner negotiates deal, then directs IRA custodian to sign purchase contract. Note: The IRA owner cannot sign the agreement because the custodian is in charge of the account and acts on behalf of the IRA owner.

4. IRA owner will locate an attorney or title company to close transaction. IRA custodian will engage and pay for these services.

5. IRA custodian will send closing proceeds from IRA to attorney or title company.

6. If financing is involved, the note must be signed by the IRA custodian. Note: Only non-recourse financing is permitted in an IRA.

7. Deed will be issued to the IRA custodian care of your IRA.

8. IRA will purchase insurance.

9. IRA owner will find a property manager for IRA custodian to engage.

10. Property manager handles all aspects of property including but not limited to collection of rents, leasing, paying expenses or taxes, repairs, etc. Property manager will send rent proceeds to IRA.

Investing in real estate through your IRA is indeed possible provided you follow a complex set of rules. Once you acquire a comfortable working knowledge of IRA investing, you may desire to invest in projects that require a more hands-on form of control due to their complexity and asset protection. Fortunately for the sophisticated investor, you can achieve this control by combining an entity with your IRA.

## ENHANCED CONTROL AND ASSET PROTECTION FOR YOUR IRA

Generally your IRA is considered an exempt asset. In Chapter 2, I explained that IRAs are referred to as exempt assets because they are protected from your personal creditors—outside liability. Generally, when it comes to investing through IRAs people will place their funds in mutual funds or stocks. These are considered safe investments from an asset protection standpoint because they do not create liability for the IRA inside liability. Real estate on the other hand is not considered a safe asset because it has the ability by itself to generate liability for its owner. This should never be overlooked when investing through your IRA.

> Sean retired early from his executive position with Boeing and elected to roll his sizable retirement fund, $2 million, into a self-directed IRA. After reviewing the success his brother Chuck enjoyed with his real estate investing, Sean decided to test the waters for himself. Chuck told John about real estate investing through an IRA, and Sean was hooked on the idea. In July, Sean's IRA took title to a small, inexpensive, three-bedroom rental in Memphis, Tennessee. Within the month, Sean's property manager had the house rented and everything was looking positive until September when Sean received notice

from his IRA custodian that his IRA was being sued by the tenant for $1,000,000.

Sean violated one of the basic tenants of asset protection—placing dangerous assets with safe assets. Most people would never consider holding real estate inside of an entity that held their savings account because this would place their savings account at risk for the real estate's liabilities. The asset protection savvy method dictates you should hold your real estate in LLCs for asset protection. This caution should not be abandoned when investing through an IRA.

In Sean's situation, he experienced firsthand how one rental house put his entire retirement account at risk. Had Sean contacted a qualified asset protection specialist, he would have been discouraged from holding title directly in the name of his IRA. Any real estate should be sheltered inside of an LLC to protect Sean's retirement funds. Remember, when investing retirement funds in non-traditional investments, the need for asset protection is amplified because your tax-free or tax-deferred monies are put at risk. However, as for all IRA strategies, knowing the law is key.

> Tired of the stock market's volatility, Sharon decided to change her investment strategy from securities to real estate. Sharon thoroughly researched real estate investing through an IRA on the Internet and discovered how important an LLC is when protecting retirement funds from real estate liabilities. Confident about her strategy, Sharon found a company on the Internet that advertised self-directed IRAs and LLCs. After contacting the company, Sharon was told by a salesman she must send a check for $2,000 to set up the LLC and fill out an application to roll over her IRA. Sharon followed his instructions, and within a month she had an LLC owned and funded by her IRA with Sharon as the manager.

Sharon made a crucial mistake by not working with an experienced IRA custodian familiar with this particular strategy. Sharon's IRA and not Sharon personally should have paid to set up the LLC. When Sharon paid the IRA custodian out of personal funds, she made an impermissible contribution to her IRA. Sharon's IRA is at risk of being disqualified.

To avoid putting your IRA at risk, you should follow a few simple rules whenever utilizing Sharon's strategy:

- The LLC should contain special provisions concerning prohibited transactions;
- The IRA and not the IRA owner must pay for the creation of the LLC. *(In my practice we will not assist in this form of transaction unless we have a signed agreement with the IRA custodian for the creation of the entity and payment is made from the IRA.);*
- The IRA will fund the LLC with IRA assets; and
- Create one IRA for each LLC and roll over enough funds for each transaction.

The last point is extremely important for enhanced IRA protection. If you decide to invest in real estate with your IRA, the possibility of a prohibited transaction occurring increases dramatically. To guard against jeopardizing all of your retirement assets, sound strategy dictates creating multiple IRAs. By dividing your IRA wealth, you limit the amount that is at risk if one IRA is disqualified because of a prohibited transaction.

After asset protection, checkbook control is the second reason given by my clients for establishing an IRA-owned LLC. Many investors do not relish the thought of dealing with their IRA custodian when it comes to completing a real estate transaction. I have heard many unfortunate stories wherein an investor was unable to close on a real estate deal because his IRA custodian was not responsive or was unable to meet the seller's timetable. The ability to close quickly when discovering a great deal is an important part of real estate investing. Take the IRA custodian out of the picture, and IRA investing becomes very attractive. As the manager of the LLC, you have the ability to control your LLC's investments. However, you must remain extremely vigilant when investing in this manner because of the increased possibility of a perceived prohibited transaction.

Caution: Many promoters of this strategy will tell you that investing through an entity owned by an IRA provides more opportunities. In other words, the same rules do not apply to entities that apply to IRAs. Again, this is the classic problem where a good idea is killed from lack of knowledge. The IRS takes the position that any activity that occurs inside of an entity owned 50% or more by an IRA is directly attributed to the IRA as if the entity did not exist. Remember Jill who bought and sold 18 properties in one year and faced taxation for running an active business through her IRA? We now know that an LLC would not offer her IRA any protection from this activity.

IRAs are not the last word in tax-deferred investing. Pension plans provide a great alternative without many of the restrictions associated with IRAs. Many people in my workshops are surprised to discover how much control and flexibility a personal pension plan can offer in terms of real estate investing, borrowing money, loaning money to the account owner, or in making contributions. After evaluating the options, I have found most people will choose a pension over an IRA, when looking to invest retirement funds in real estate properties. To find out more on creating your own pension plan, contact my office for a free consultation.

# Case Studies

## Background

- Married with no children
- Residents of California
- Husband and wife both work for a local municipality
- Husband plans to quit his job and invest in real estate full-time in Southern California.

### CASE STUDY 1

- ▶ Married Couple
- ▶ Beginning Investor
- ▶ Low Risk

#### ASSETS

| ASSET | FMV | DEBT | EQUITY |
|---|---|---|---|
| Personal Residence | $600,000 | $450,000 | $150,000 |
| Vehicles | $45,000 | $0 | $45,000 |
| Personal Property | $35,000 | $0 | $35,000 |
| Cash/Savings | $15,000 | $0 | $15,000 |
| IRA | $8,000 | $0 | $8,000 |

- Primary investing strategy for foreseeable future will be buying and selling distressed properties and wholesaling for quick cash flow.

## Analysis

These investors are just getting started, so it is safe to assume that they will have some startup expenses, e.g., education, research, computer, etc. Further, the nature of their investing will be short-term. Investing in their own name could open them up to liability and dealer status.

**Corporation**—A corporation will isolate the investors from dealer status and formalize their investing business. With a formal business structure, the investors will deduct the various expenses associated with their real estate activities.

The question of where to create this corporation should be based on where the investing activity will occur. These investors indicated their intent to invest in Southern California. If this will hold true for the foreseeable future, then a corporation organized in California will be appropriate.

**Living Trust**—The various other assets owned by the investors, with the exception of the IRA, should be placed in a joint living trust. It is neither necessary nor advisable to create an asset protection entity for the personal property or the savings at this time. Personal property should never be held in an asset protection entity because of its personal and non-business nature, and the investors' cash and savings are not yet at a threshold to warrant the creation of an entity for protection of these assets. Similarly, the vehicles should be held by the living trust unless a vehicle is utilized solely for business.

## Background

- Single
- Resident of Oklahoma
- Sole-proprietor website designer—works out of home
- Primary investing strategy will be to find distressed sellers and then purchase their property subject to an existing mortgage.

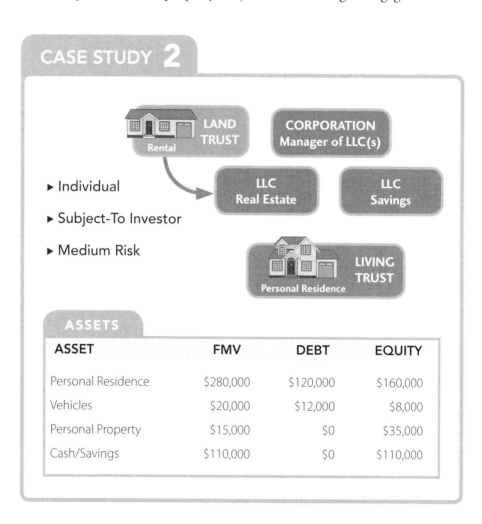

## Analysis

This investment strategy has some unique components because the investor is purchasing property from distressed sellers and then finding tenants to acquire the property under a lease option. The opportunity to acquire property with little money down and to use another person's credit makes this form of investing very popular. The challenge for the investor is to take title without alerting the bank that title was transferred.

**Land Trust**—A land trust will be utilized to take title to the property from a distressed seller. The land trust will hold title to the property with the distressed seller as the beneficiary and the investor as the trustee. The seller will transfer his property into the trust by recoding a deed naming the trust as the Grantee. After the property is recorded into the trust, the investor (actually an LLC owned and controlled by the investor) will purchase the seller's beneficial interest.

**Limited Liability Company**—Because of the risk associated with rental properties, the investor should hold each property he acquires, either directly or indirectly through a land trust, in a separate LLC for asset protection. Another LLC should be established to hold the investor's ample savings account. This LLC will protect liquid assets from the investor's personal creditors. If any of these funds are needed for property acquisitions, the investor can borrow from his LLC and give the LLC a deed trust against one of his properties as security for the loan. This technique is commonly referred to as equity stripping.

The LLCs can be set up as disregarded entities for federal tax purposes because the investor is the sole member of each LLC. A corporation can be established to manage each of the LLCs. Each of the LLCs should be established in Oklahoma because this is where the investing will occur.

**Corporation**—A corporation would make sense as the manager for each LLC created by the investor. The corporation should also be used for the investor's website business. The investor is a sole proprietor for all of the website work. A sole proprietor is subject to employment taxes on the first $100,000 of earnings. This can amount to more than $14,000 each year. As a corporation, the investor can take a reasonable salary (subject to employment taxes) and a dividend (not subject to employment taxes), effectively reducing his overall tax rate and providing liability protection for his business. Because the management activity and the website design take place in Oklahoma, this corporation should be established in Oklahoma.

**Living Trust**—A living trust should be created to hold the investor's personal residence, LLC, and corporate business interests, vehicles, and all personal effects. A living trust will bypass probate and ensure an orderly distribution of the investor's assets upon his passing.

## Background

- Husband runs the remodel site work while the wife manages their home office and raises their three children ages 8, 14, and 17.
- Residents of Florida
- It is not uncommon for these investors to have three properties under remodel at any given time. To complete projects on a timely basis, the investors have a four-man crew that works alongside the husband.

## CASE STUDY 3

- Married Couple
- Property Rehabber
- High Risk

### ASSETS

| ASSET | FMV | DEBT | EQUITY |
|---|---|---|---|
| Personal Residence | $1,000,000 | $0 | $1,000,000 |
| Vehicles | $120,000 | $0 | $120,000 |
| Personal Property | $95,000 | $0 | $95,000 |
| Cash/Savings | $175,000 | $0 | $175,000 |

## Analysis

This investor has a substantial amount of risk exposure ranging from employees, remodeled properties, and two teenage children. Each of these threats must be addressed in their plan.

**Corporation**—A Florida corporation should be established to conduct all of the remodeling activities. The corporation will be owned and operated by the husband and wife. When the husband finds a new property to remodel, he will purchase the property with his corporation and perform the necessary work. His four-man crew will become employees of the corporation. Careful consideration should be given to the number of rehabs being performed at one time by the corporation. If a rehab were to suddenly burn down or to create some other liability for the corporation, each of the other properties would be at risk.

**Limited Liability Company**—Three Florida LLCs should be created. One LLC will hold their savings account and the others their rehabs. The husband and wife will own the savings LLC. Their corporation will own 100% of the rehab LLCs. The rehabs should be divided between the LLCs to minimize the overall risk exposure from the rehab business. All profit and loss from each property will flow to the corporation as the single member of each LLC.

A fourth LLC might be considered to hold any business assets, i.e. vehicles, tools, equipment, etc., used by the corporation to conduct its business. The LLC will lease the equipment to the corporation for a reasonable fee.

**Living Trust**—A joint living trust should be created to hold the husband and wife's personal residence, LLC, corporate business interests, vehicles, and all personal effects. Although there is a significant amount of equity in the couple's personal residence, Florida provides an unlimited homestead exemption. When placing the residence into their living trust, the couple must reserve this exemption in the deed. The living trust can provide for distribution of the couple's estate through trusts to the children.

## Background

- Husband and wife have no children.
- Residents of Colorado
- Husband works for Postal Service and wife is a dental hygienist.

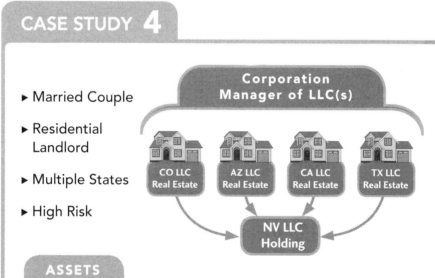

### CASE STUDY 4

- Married Couple
- Residential Landlord
- Multiple States
- High Risk

#### ASSETS

| ASSET | FMV | DEBT | EQUITY |
|---|---|---|---|
| Personal Residence | $800,000 | $750,000 | $50,000 |
| Vehicles | $35,000 | $10,000 | $25,000 |
| 3 Colorado Rentals | $775,000 | $600,000 | $175,000 |
| Arizona Rental | $500,000 | $495,000 | $5,000 |
| 2 California Condos | $475,000 | $275,000 | $200,000 |
| 5 Texas Rentals | $650,000 | $300,000 | $350,000 |
| Cash/Savings | $25,000 | $0 | $25,000 |

## Analysis

This couple has exposure from their multiple rental properties and from the wife's profession. Even though the couple is resides in Colorado, their real estate investing is nationwide. To manage their out-of-state properties, the couple employs local property management companies.

**Limited Liability Company**—The optimal asset protection structure would utilize one LLC per property; however, to limit costs the couple might consider one Colorado LLC, one California LLC, and two Texas LLCs. This strategy would limit their overall equity exposure to less than $200,000 per LLC. As the equity grows, the couple can remove specific properties and place them into new LLCs.

Because the couple resides in a non–community property state, each LLC will be taxed as a partnership if both husband and wife desire an ownership interest in the LLCs. To avoid filing three partnership returns, the couple might elect to form a Nevada LLC to hold the interest of each property LLC. In forming the Nevada LLC, the couple can file the other LLCs as single-member disregarded entities (no federal tax returns) and the Nevada LLC will provide the couple with enhanced asset protection at the member level. Protection at the membership level is extremely important given the wife's higher-risk profession.

**Corporation**—A corporation should be considered if the couple is actively involved in managing their local rentals. If the properties produce positive income, then a corporation could provide some tax benefits and liability protection for the couple when it comes to their property management activities. If the couple decides to create a Nevada LLC, then they should file their corporation in Nevada and then register it in each state where they conduct rental activity. The corporation will serve as the manager of each LLC.

**Land Trust**—If the couple is concerned about the due-on-sale clause in their mortgage agreements, they should utilize a land trust for each LLC. The land trust would hold title to the rental units and the LLC would be the trust beneficiary. For anonymity purposes, the couple should consider using their attorney to serve as the trustee of each of their trusts.

**Living Trust**—A joint living trust should be created to hold the couple's personal residence, LLC, corporate business interests, vehicles, and all personal effects.

## Background

- Investor is single with two grown children.
- Resident of California
- Investor purchases tracts of distressed land throughout the United States and holds them until market conditions

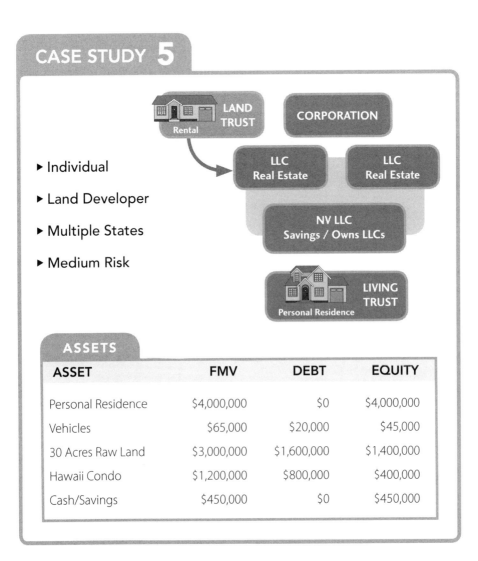

### CASE STUDY 5

- Individual
- Land Developer
- Multiple States
- Medium Risk

### ASSETS

| ASSET | FMV | DEBT | EQUITY |
|---|---|---|---|
| Personal Residence | $4,000,000 | $0 | $4,000,000 |
| Vehicles | $65,000 | $20,000 | $45,000 |
| 30 Acres Raw Land | $3,000,000 | $1,600,000 | $1,400,000 |
| Hawaii Condo | $1,200,000 | $800,000 | $400,000 |
| Cash/Savings | $450,000 | $0 | $450,000 |

improve. When the investor believes it is time to sell, he will subdivide the land into lots for sale to other developers or for personal development.

## Analysis

This investor is at risk of being classified as a dealer. As a dealer, he cannot qualify for long-term capital gains treatment when he sells property held for more than one year. The investor has a considerable amount of assets exposed outside of his land investments.

**Limited Liability Company**—The land and condo should be placed in separate LLCs established in the state where the property is located. Each LLC will be a single-member disregarded entity. When the investor is ready to subdivide the land and/or develop it, he should sell the undivided parcel to his corporation. The sale will result in long-term capital gains treatment if the property is held for more than a year and the developer did not begin development of the property.

A separate Nevada LLC should be established to hold the investor's savings. The Nevada LLC will provide superior asset protection for the investor's liquid assets in addition to providing anonymity.

**Corporation**—A corporation should be utilized for land development. If the investor develops property in his own name, he will be classified as a dealer. To avoid dealer status and to minimize his taxes, the corporation will perform all development activity.

**Land Trust**—Hawaii recognizes land trust by statute. If the investor is concerned that his lender will exercise the due-on-sale clause when the condo is transferred into an LLC, then a land trust should be created. The land trust would hold title to the condo, and the LLC would be the trust beneficiary. For anonymity purposes, the investor should consider using his attorney to serve as the trustee of the land trust.

**Living Trust**—A living trust should be created to hold the investor's personal residence, LLCs, corporate business interests, vehicles, and all personal effects.

## Background

- Two friends, each is married to someone else outside the business.
- Residents of Texas
- Friends/investors pool their resources and invest in real estate in their local market. The investors each hold a 50% interest

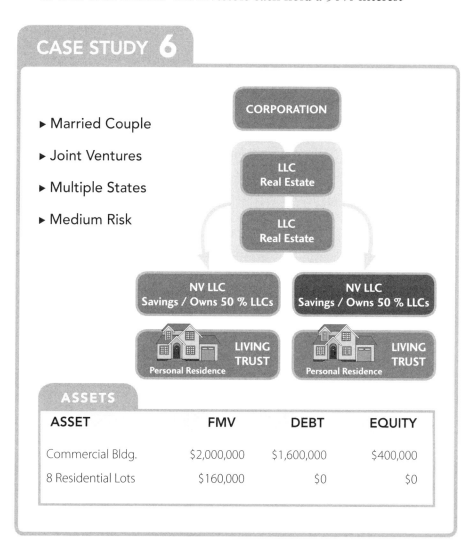

in each project. Presently they own a commercial building and residential lots for future development. They plan to acquire additional commercial properties over the next few years.

## Analysis

Each investor holds his 50% interest in his own name. The investors are exposed to real estate liabilities and the risks associated with co-ownership.

**Limited Liability Company**—The lots should be placed in an LLC established in the state where the property is located. Each LLC will be considered a partnership for federal tax purposes because the LLC will have two owners. Similarly, the investors should establish an LLC to hold their commercial real estate investment.

Each investor should establish a separate LLC (holding LLC) to hold their jointly held LLC interests. Because the investors reside in a community property state, each separate LLC could be established as a disregarded entity for federal tax purposes. The separate holding LLC will insulate the jointly held LLCs from each investor's personal liabilities.

**Corporation**—A corporation should be considered when additional properties are acquired to centrally manage their various investments. Each investor will own the corporation equally.

**Land Trust**—Not needed because the land trust does not offer due-on-sale clause protection for encumbered commercial real estate.

**Living Trust**—Each investor should establish a joint living trust to hold their respective personal residences, LLC interests, vehicles, and all personal effects.

# Homestead Laws

**Alabama**—Up to $5,000 in value, or up to 160 acres in area.—Code of Alabama, § 6-10-2

**Alaska**—Up to $64,800 in value, no area limitation.—Alaska Statutes, § 09.39.010

**Arizona**—Up to $100,000 in value, no area limitation—Arizona Revised Statutes, § 33-1101

**Arkansas**—Up to $2,500 in value, or at least ¼ acre for city homesteads, 80 acres for rural homesteads—Arkansas Code, §§ 16- 66- 210 and 218; Arkansas Constitution Article 9

**California**—Up to $50,000 in value—California Code Annotated, § 704.730

**Colorado**—Up to $45,000 in value, no area limitation—Colorado Revised Statutes Annotated, § 38-41-201

**Connecticut**—Up to $75,000 in value, no area limitation—Connecticut General Statutes Annotated, § 52-352b

**Delaware**—None—provided Delaware Code Annotated, § 4901-3

**District of Columbia**—D. C. provides an exemption equal to owner's aggregate interest in real property (No monetary or area limitations) -District of Columbia Code § 15- 501. DC does not call this a homestead exemption

**Florida**—Exemption equal to value of property as assessed for tax purposes (No monetary limitations)—area limitations of ½ acre urban land or 160 acres rural land—Florida Constitution, Article 10 § 4

**Georgia**—Up to $5,000 in value, no area limitation. Code of Georgia, Annotated, § 44-13-1 and 44-13-100

**Hawaii**—Up to $20,000 in value, but the head of a family and persons 65 years of age or older are allowed up to $30,000, no area limitation—Hawaii Revised Statutes §§ 651-91, 92

**Idaho**—Up to $50,000 in value, no area limitation—Idaho Code § 55- 1003

**Illinois**—Up to $7,500 in value, no area limitation. Where multiple owners, can be increased to $15,000—Illinois Compiled Statutes, Annotated, § 734 5/12-901

**Indiana**—Up to $7,500 in value for residence, up to $4,000 for additional property, no area limitation. Co-owner, if also a joint debtor, may claim additional $7,500. Annotated Indiana Code, § 34-55-10-2

**Iowa**—No monetary limitation, but a minimum value of $500— area limitations of ½ acre urban land or 40 acres rural land— Iowa Code Annotated, §§ 561.2 and 561.16

**Kansas**—No monetary limitation—area limitations of 1 acre urban land or 160 acres rural land—Kansas Constitution, Article 15 § 9 and Kansas Statutes, Annotated, § 60-2301

**Kentucky**—Up to $5,000 in value, no area limitation—Kentucky Revised Statutes, § 427.060

**Louisiana**—Up to $25,000 in value, but may include entirety of property in cases of catastrophic or terminal illness or injury. Area limitations of 5 acres urban land or 200 acres rural land—Louisiana Statutes Annotated, § 20:1

**Maine**—Up to $25,000 in value, but may be up to $60,000 under certain circumstances, no area limitation—Maine Revised Statutes, Annotated, §4422

**Maryland**—Up to $3,000 in value, but in Title XI bankruptcy proceedings up to $2,500, no area limitation—Annotated Code of Maryland, § 11-504

**Massachusetts**—Up to $300,000 in value, no area limitation—Annotated Laws of Massachusetts, § 188-1

**Michigan**—Up to $3,500 in value, area limitations of 1 acre urban land or 40 acres rural land—Michigan Compiled Laws, § 600.6023

**Minnesota**—Up to $200,000 in value, but up to $500,000 if used primarily for agricultural purposes, area limitations of ½ acre urban land or 160 acres rural land—Minnesota Statutes, Annotated, §510.02

**Mississippi**—Up to $75,000 in value, area limitation of 160 acres—Annotated Mississippi Code, § 85-3-21

**Missouri**—Up to $8,000 in value, no area limitation—Annotated Missouri Statutes, § 513.475

**Montana**—Up to $100,000 in value, no area limitation—Montana Code, Annotated, §§ 70-32-101, 70-32-104, and 70-32-201

**Nebraska**—Up to $12,500 in value, area limitation of 2 lots, urban land or 160 acres rural land—Revised Statutes of Nebraska, § 40-101

**Nevada**—Up to $125,000 in equity, no area limitation—Nevada Revised Statutes, § 115-010

**New Hampshire**—Up to $50,000 in value, no area limitation—New Hampshire Revised Statutes, Annotated, § 480:1

**New Jersey**—No homestead exemption is provided, but an exemption for personal property of up to $1,000 is allowed—New Jersey Statutes, Annotated, § 2A:17-1 and 2A:17-17

**New Mexico**—Up to $30,000 in value, no area limitation—New Mexico Statutes, Annotated, § 2-10-9

**New York**—Up to $10,000 above liens and encumbrances in value, no area limitation—Consolidated Laws of New York, Annotated, CPLR § 5206

**North Carolina**—Up to $10,000 in value, no area limitation—General Statutes of North Carolina, Annotated, §1C-1601 and North Carolina Constitution, Article X

**North Dakota**—Up to $80,000 in value, no area limitation—North Dakota Century Code, Annotated, § 47-18-01

**Ohio**—Up to $5,000 in value, no area limitation—Ohio Revised Code, § 2329.66

**Oklahoma**—Unlimited in value, area limitations of 1 acre urban land or 160 acres rural land. However, where using more than 25% of property for business purpose, the value drops to $5,000—Oklahoma Statutes, Annoted, §§ 1 and 2

**Oregon**—Up to $25,000 in value, area limitations of one city block if within a city or 160 acres rural land—Oregon Revised Statutes, § 23.240

**Pennsylvania**—No homestead exemption provided, but a general monetary exemption of $300 exists—Pennsylvania Consolidated Statutes, Annotated, §§ 8121, et. Seq.

**Rhode Island**—Up to $150,000 in value, no area limitation—General Laws of Rhode Island, § 9-26-4.1

**South Carolina**—Although no homestead exemption is provided, an exemption for personal and real property of up to $10,000 in value may include property claimed as a residence—Code of Laws of South Carolina, § 15-41-30

**South Dakota**—No monetary limitation, area limitation of one dwelling house and contiguous lots used in good faith—South Dakota Codified Laws, §§ 43-31-1 and 43-31-4

**Tennessee**—Up to $5,000, but may be up to $7,500 if claimed by two persons as a homestead, no area limitation—Tennessee Code, Annotated, § 26-2-301

**Texas**—No monetary limitation, area limitation of 10 acres urban land or 100 acres of rural land if claimed by a single person. A family may claim 200 acres of rural land—Texas Property Code, Annotated, §§ 41.001 and 41.002 and Texas Constitution, Article 16 § 51

**Utah**—Up to $20,000 in value, but only $5,000 in value if property is not primary residence, area limitation of 1 acre—Utah Code, § 78-23-3

**Vermont**—Up to $75,000 in value, no area limitation—Vermont Statutes Annotated, Title 27, § 101

**Virginia**—Up to $5,000, but may be increased by $500 for each dependent residing on property, no area limitation—Code of Virginia, § 34-4

**Washington**—Generally, up to $40,000 in value, but may be unlimited if used against income taxes on retirement plan benefits, no area limitation—Revised Code of Washington, Annotated, § 6.13.030

**West Virginia**—Up to $5,000 in value, but an additional $7,500 may be available in cases of "catastrophic illness or injury," no area limitation—West Virginia Code, Annotated, §§ 38-9-1 and 38-10-4

**Wisconsin**—Up to $40,000 in value, no area limitation—Wisconsin Statutes, Annotated, § 815.20

**Wyoming**—Up to $10,000 in value, each co-owner is entitled to a homestead exemption—Wyoming Statutes § 1-20-101

# Overview of State LLC Asset Protection Laws

## Alabama Judgment Creditor Remedy

**LIMITED PARTNERSHIP:**

Under the Alabama Limited Partnership Act, the court may charge the debtor-partner's partnership interest with payment of unsatisfied judgments. The judgment creditor is treated as an assignee of the debtor-partner's transferable interest. However, under the statue the **charging order is not the exclusive remedy.**

### Section 10-9B-703

Rights of creditor

On application to a court of competent jurisdiction by any judgment creditor of a partner, the court may charge the partnership interest of the partner with payment of the unsatisfied amount of the judgment with interest. To the extent so charged, the judgment creditor has only the rights of an assignee of the partnership interest. This chapter does not deprive any partner of the benefit of any exemption laws applicable to his or her partnership interest.

*(Act 97-921, 1st Ex. Sess., p. 335, &sect; 1.)*

**LIMITED LIABILITY COMPANY:**

Under the Alabama Limited Liability Company Act the **charging order is the exclusive remedy**.

### Section 10-12-35

*(Applicable to limited liability companies organized after January 1, 1998, limited liability companies not electing to come under the pre-*

1997 changes, and to all limited liability companies after December 31, 2000.) Member's financial rights subject to charging order.

(a) On application to a court of competent jurisdiction by any judgment creditor of a member or assignee, the court may charge the interest of the member or assignee with payment of the unsatisfied amount of the judgment with interest. To the extent so charged, the judgment creditor has only the rights of an assignee of financial rights. **This section shall be the sole and exclusive remedy of a judgment creditor with respect to the judgment debtor's membership interest.**

(b) This chapter does not deprive any member of the benefit of any exemption laws applicable to the member's limited liability company interest.

(Acts 1993, No. 93-724, p. 1425, &sect;35; Act 97-920, 1st Ex. Sess., p. 312, &sect;1.)

## Alaska Judgment Creditor Remedy

### LIMITED PARTNERSHIPS:

Under the Alaska Uniform Partnership Act a transferee of a partner or a judgment creditor's **exclusive remedy is a charging order** placed on the debtor-partner's partnership interest. The charging order constitutes a lien on the debtor-partner's transferable interest in the partnership.

#### Sec. 32.11.340 Rights of creditor

(a) On application to a court of competent jurisdiction by a judgment creditor of a partner, the court may charge the partnership interest of the partner with payment of the unsatisfied amount of the judgment with interest. To the extent charged, the judgment creditor has only the rights of an assignee of the partnership interest. This chapter does not deprive a partner of the benefit of an exemption law applicable to the partner's partnership interest.

(b) **This section provides the exclusive remedy that a judgment creditor of a general or limited partner or of the general or limited partner's assignee may use to satisfy a judgment out of the judgment debtor's interest in the partnership.** Other remedies, including foreclosure on the general or limited partner's partnership interest and a court order for directions, accounts, and inquiries that the debtor general or limited partner might have made, are not available to the judgment creditor attempting to satisfy the judgment out of the judgment debtor's interest in the limited partnership and may not be ordered by a court.

## LIMITED LIABILITY COMPANIES:

Under Alaska's Revised Limited Liability Company Act, a judgment credit may charge the debtor-member's limited liability company with interest of any unsatisfied amount of debt. This is the **judgment creditor's exclusive remedy**. The judgment creditor has only the rights of an assignee of the debtor-member's interest.

### Sec. 10.50.380 Rights of judgment creditors

(a) If a judgment creditor of a limited liability company member applies to a court of competent jurisdiction, the court may charge the member's limited liability company interest for payment of the unsatisfied amount of the judgment.

(b) To the extent a limited liability company interest is charged under (a) of this section, the judgment creditor has only the rights of an assignee of the member's interest.

(c) **This section provides the exclusive remedy** that a judgment creditor of a member or a member's assignee may use to satisfy a judgment out of the judgment debtor's interest in the limited liability company. Other remedies, including foreclosure on the member's limited liability company interest and a court order for directions, accounts, and inquiries that the debtor member might have made, are not available to the judgment creditor attempting to satisfy a judgment out of the judgment debtor's interest in the limited liability company and may not be ordered by a court.

(d) This section does not deprive a member of the benefit of an exemption applicable to the member's membership interest.

# Arizona Judgment Creditor Remedy

## LIMITED PARTNERSHIPS:

Upon petition by a judgment creditor the court may enter, as the **judgment creditor's exclusive remedy**, a charging order charging the debtor-partner's partnership interest with payment of unsatisfied amount of the judgment.

### 29-341 Rights of judgment creditor

On application to a court of competent jurisdiction by any judgment creditor of a partner, the court may charge the partnership interest of the partner with payment of the unsatisfied amount of the judgment with interest. To the extent so charged, the judgment creditor has only the rights of an assignee of the partner's partnership interest. This chapter does not deprive any partner of the benefit of any exemption laws applicable to his partnership interest. **This section provides the exclusive remedy by which a judgment creditor of a partner may satisfy a judgment out of the judgment debtor's interest in the partnership.**

### LIMITED LIABILITY COMPANIES:

Under Arizona's Limited Liability Company Act, a judgment creditor may ask the court to charge the member's interest in the LLC with payment of an unsatisfied amount with interest. The judgment creditor receives only the rights of an assignee of the member's interest in the LLC. This is the **judgment creditor's exclusive remedy.**

#### 29-655 Rights of judgment creditors of a member

A. On application to a court of competent jurisdiction by any judgment creditor of a member, the court may charge the member's interest in the limited liability company with payment of the unsatisfied amount of the judgment plus interest. To the extent so charged, the judgment creditor has only the rights of an assignee of the member's interest.

B. This chapter does not deprive any member of the benefit of any exemption laws applicable to his interest in the limited liability company.

C. **This section provides the exclusive remedy by which a judgment creditor of a member may satisfy a judgment out of the judgment debtor's interest in the limited liability company.**

## Arkansas Judgment Creditor Remedy

### LIMITED PARTNERSHIPS:

Under the Revised Limited Partnership Act (1991), a judgment creditor may charge a debtor-partner's transferable partnership interest with payment of any unsatisfied amount. The judgment creditor receives only the rights of an assignee, however, **the court may order foreclosure on the interest.**

### 4-46-504 Partner's transferable interest subject to charging order

(a) On application by a judgment creditor of a partner or of a partner's transferee, a court having jurisdiction may charge the transferable interest of the judgment debtor to satisfy the judgment. The court may appoint a receiver of the share of the distributions due or to become due to the judgment debtor in respect of the partnership and make all other orders, directions, accounts, and inquiries the judgment debtor might have made or which the circumstances of the case may require.
(b) A charging order constitutes a lien on the judgment debtor's transferable interest in the partnership. **The court may order a foreclosure of the interest subject to the charging order at any time.** The purchaser at the foreclosure sale has the rights of a transferee.
(c) At any time before foreclosure, an interest charged may be redeemed:
   (1) by the judgment debtor;
   (2) with property other than partnership property, by one (1) or more of the other partners; or
   (3) with partnership property, by one (1) or more of the other partners with the consent of all of the partners whose interests are not so charged.
(d) This chapter does not deprive a partner of a right under exemption laws with respect to the partner's interest in the partnership.
(e) This section provides the exclusive remedy by which a judgment creditor of a partner or partner's transferee may satisfy a judgment out of the judgment debtor's transferable interest in the partnership.

## LIMITED LIABILITY COMPANIES:

The judgment creditor receives the rights of the assignee in the amount of judgment on the debtor-member's membership interest, however, **the statute does not say that this is judgment creditor's exclusive remedy**. Click here to view the statute.

### 4-32-705 Rights of judgment creditor

On application to a court of competent jurisdiction by any judgment creditor of a member, the court may charge the member's limited liability company interest with payment of the unsatisfied amount of judgment with interest. To the extent so charged, the judgment creditor has only the rights of an assignee of the member's limited liability company interest. This chapter does not deprive any member of the benefit of any exemption laws applicable to his or her limited liability company interest.

# California Judgment Creditor Remedy

**LIMITED PARTNERSHIPS:**

California's Uniform Partnership Act authorizes **foreclosure of a partner's charged interest** without the consent of the other partners.

### Cal. Corp. Code Section 16504

(a) On application by a judgment creditor of a partner or of a partner's transferee, a court having jurisdiction may charge the transferable interest of the judgment debtor to satisfy the judgment. The court may appoint a receiver of the share of the distributions due or to become due to the judgment debtor in respect of the partnership and make all other orders, directions, accounts, and inquiries the judgment debtor might have made or that thecircumstances of the case may require.

(b) A charging order constitutes a lien on the judgment debtor's transferable interest in the partnership. The court may order a foreclosure of the interest subject to the charging order at any time. The purchaser at the foreclosure sale has the rights of a transferee.

(c) At any time before foreclosure, an interest charged may be redeemed in any of the following manners:

(1) By the judgment debtor.

(2) With property other than partnership property, by one or more of the other partners.

(3) With partnership property, by one or more of the other partners with the consent of all of the partners whose interests are not so charged.

(d) This chapter does not deprive a partner of a right under exemption laws with respect to the partner's interest in the partnership.

(e) This section provides the exclusive remedy by which a judgment creditor of a partner or partner's transferee may satisfy a judgment out of the judgment debtor's transferable interest in the partnership.

## LIMITED LIABILITY COMPANIES:

California law allows the courts to **foreclose on the member's interest** subject to the charging order.

### Cal. Corp. Code Section 17302

(a) On application by a judgment creditor of a member or of a member's assignee, a court having jurisdiction may charge the assignable membership interest of the judgment debtor to satisfy the judgment. The court may appoint a receiver of the share of the distributions due or to become due to the judgment debtor in respect to the limited liability company and may make all other orders, directions, accounts, and inquiries that the judgment debtor might have made or that the circumstances of the case may require.

(b) A charging order constitutes a lien on the judgment debtor's assignable membership interest. **The court may order a foreclosure on the membership interest subject to the charging order at any time.** The purchaser at the foreclosure sale has the rights of an assignee.

(c) At any time before foreclosure, a membership interest charged may be redeemed in any of the following manners:

  (1) By the judgment debtor.

  (2) With property other than property of the limited liability company by one or more of the other members.

  (3) With property of the limited liability company by one or more of the other members with the consent of all of the members whose membership interests are not so charged.

(d) This section does not deprive any member or assignee of a membership interest of the benefit of any exemption laws applicable to the membership interest in the limited liability company.

(e) This section provides the exclusive remedy by which a judgment creditor of a member or of a member's assignee may satisfy a judgment out of the judgment debtor's membership interest in the limited liability company.

# Colorado Judgment Creditor Remedy

## LIMITED PARTNERSHIPS:

A judgment creditor may seek to charge the debtor-partner's partnership interest with payment of any unsatisfied judgments. However, **this is not the judgment creditor's exclusive remedy.**

## LIMITED LIABILITY COMPANIES:

The court may charge the membership interest of the member with payment of unsatisfied amount of the judgment with interest theron and may then or later appoint a receiver of the member's share of the profits and any other money due or to become due to the member in respect of the limited liability company and make all other order, directions, accounts, and inquires that the debtor member might have made. **Charging order is not the exclusive remedy.**

# Connecticut Judgment Creditor Remedy

## LIMITED PARTNERSHIPS:

Under Connecticut statutes a**judicial foreclosure is a remedy.**

### Sec. 34-349 Partner's transferable interest subject to charging order

(a) On application by a judgment creditor of a partner or of a partner's transferee, a court having jurisdiction may charge the transferable interest of the judgment debtor to satisfy the judgment. The court may appoint a receiver of the share of the distributions due or to become due to the judgment debtor in respect of the partnership and make all other orders, directions, accounts, and inquiries the judgment debtor might have made or which the circumstances of the case may require.

(b) A charging order constitutes a lien on the judgment debtor's transferable interest in the partnership. The court may order a foreclosure of the interest subject to the charging order at any time. The purchaser at the foreclosure sale has the rights of a transferee.

(c) At any time before foreclosure, an interest charged may be redeemed: (1) By the judgment debtor; (2) with property other than partnership property, by one or more of the other partners; or (3) with partnership property, by one or more of the other partners with the consent of all of the partners whose interests are not so charged.

(d) Sections 34-300 to 34-399, inclusive, do not deprive a partner of a right under exemption laws with respect to the partner's interest in the partnership.

*Appendix B: Overview of State LLC Asset Protection Laws*     175

(e) This section provides the exclusive remedy by which a judgment creditor of a partner or partner's transferee may satisfy a judgment out of the judgment debtor's transferable interest in the partnership.

## LIMITED LIABILITY COMPANIES:

The Connecticut statute **does not list the charging order as the exclusive remedy**.

### Sec. 34-171 Rights of judgment creditor

On application to a court of competent jurisdiction by any judgment creditor of a member, the court may charge the member's limited liability company interest with payment of the unsatisfied amount of the judgment with interest. To the extent so charged, the judgment creditor has only the rights of an assignee of the member's limited liability company interest. Nothing in sections 34-100 to 34-242, inclusive, shall be held to deprive a member of the benefit of any exemption provided by law applicable to such person's limited liability company membership interest.

# Delaware Judgment Creditor Remedy

## LIMITED PARTNERSHIPS:

Under the Delaware Revised Uniform Partnership Act and Revised Uniform Limited Partnership Act a **charging order is the judgment creditor's exclusive remedy**.

### § 17-703 Partner's partnership interest subject to charging order

(a) On application by a judgment creditor of a partner or of a partner's assignee, a court having jurisdiction may charge the partnership interest of the judgment debtor to satisfy the judgment. To the extent so charged, the judgment creditor has only the right to receive any distribution or distributions to which the judgment debtor would otherwise have been entitled in respect of such partnership interest.

(b) A charging order constitutes a lien on the judgment debtor's partnership interest.

(c) This chapter does not deprive a partner or partner's assignee of a right under exemption laws with respect to the judgment debtor's partnership interest.

**(d) The entry of a charging order is the exclusive remedy by**

which a judgment creditor of a partner or of a partner's assignee may satisfy a judgment out of the judgment debtor's partnership interest.

(e) No creditor of a partner or of a partner's assignee shall have any right to obtain possession of, or otherwise exercise legal or equitable remedies with respect to, the property of the limited partnership.

(f) The Court of Chancery shall have jurisdiction to hear and determine any matter relating to any such charging order.

( 6 Del. C. 1953, § 1722; 59 Del. Laws, c. 105, § 1; 63 Del. Laws, c. 420, § 1; 65 Del. Laws, c. 188, § 1; 70 Del. Laws, c. 186, § 1; 72 Del. Laws, c. 386, § 23; 75 Del. Laws, c. 31, §§ 10-16.; )

## LIMITED LIABILITY COMPANIES:

Under Delaware's Limited Liability Company Act, a judgment creditor of a member or a member's assignee may charge the limited liability company interest of the judgment debtor to satisfy a judgment. This charging order will constitute a lien on the judgment debtor-member's limited liability company interest. This is the judgment creditor's **exclusive remedy**.

### § 18-703 Member's limited liability company interest subject to charging order

(a) On application by a judgment creditor of a member or of a member's assignee, a court having jurisdiction may charge the limited liability company interest of the judgment debtor to satisfy the judgment. To the extent so charged, the judgment creditor has only the right to receive any distribution or distributions to which the judgment debtor would otherwise have been entitled in respect of such limited liability company interest.

(b) A charging order constitutes a lien on the judgment debtor's limited liability company interest.

(c) This chapter does not deprive a member or member's assignee of a right under exemption laws with respect to the judgment debtor's limited liability company interest.

(d) **The entry of a charging order is the exclusive remedy by which a judgment creditor of a member or of a member's assignee may satisfy a judgment out of the judgment debtor's limited liability company interest.**

(e) No creditor of a member or of a member's assignee shall have any right to obtain possession of, or otherwise exercise legal or equitable remedies with respect to, the property of the limited liability company.

(f) The Court of Chancery shall have jurisdiction to hear and determine any matter relating to any such charging order.

( 68 Del. Laws, c. 434, § 1; 70 Del. Laws, c. 186, § 1; 72 Del. Laws, c. 389, § 24; 75 Del. Laws, c. 51, §§ 9-15.; )

## Florida Judgment Creditor Remedy

### LIMITED PARTNERSHIPS:

Under Florida Statutes a judgment creditor is entitled to a charging order against a debtor-partner; once this charging order is secured the creditor has only the rights of an assignee of the partnership interest. This is the **exclusive remedy**.

**620.1703 Rights of creditor of partner or transferee**

(1) On application to a court of competent jurisdiction by any judgment creditor of a partner or transferee, the court may charge the partnership interest of the partner or transferable interest of a transferee with payment of the unsatisfied amount of the judgment with interest. To the extent so charged, the judgment creditor has only the rights of a transferee of the partnership interest.

(2) This act shall not deprive any partner or transferee of the benefit of an exemption law applicable to the partner's partnership or transferee's transferable interest.

(3) **This section provides the exclusive remedy which a judgment creditor of a partner or transferee may use to satisfy a judgment out of the judgment debtor's interest in the limited partnership or transferable interest.** Other remedies, including foreclosure on the partner's interest in the limited partnership or a transferee's transferable interest and a court order for directions, accounts, and inquiries that the debtor general or limited partner might have made, are not available to the judgment creditor attempting to satisfy the judgment out of the judgment debtor's interest in the limited partnership and may not be ordered by a court.

**History.**--s. 17, ch. 2005-267.

## LIMITED LIABILITY COMPANIES:

A charging order is permitted in Florida; however, **it is not the judgment creditor's exclusive remedy.**

### 608.433 Right of assignee to become member

(1) Unless otherwise provided in the articles of organization or operating agreement, an assignee of a limited liability company interest may become a member only if all members other than the member assigning the interest consent.

(2) An assignee who has become a member has, to the extent assigned, the rights and powers, and is subject to the restrictions and liabilities, of the assigning member under the articles of organization, the operating agreement, and this chapter. An assignee who becomes a member also is liable for the obligations of the assignee's assignor to make and return contributions as provided in s. 608.4211 and wrongful distributions as provided in s. 608.428. However, the assignee is not obligated for liabilities which are unknown to the assignee at the time the assignee became a member and which could not be ascertained from the articles of organization or the operating agreement.

(3) If an assignee of a limited liability company interest becomes a member, the assignor is not released from liability to the limited liability company under ss. 608.4211, 608.4228, and 608.426.

(4) On application to a court of competent jurisdiction by any judgment creditor of a member, the court may charge the limited liability company membership interest of the member with payment of the unsatisfied amount of the judgmentwith interest. **To the extent so charged, the judgment creditor has only the rights of an assignee of such interest.** This chapter does not deprive any member of the benefit of any exemption laws applicable to the member's interest.

# Georgia Judgment Creditor Remedy

## LIMITED PARTNERSHIPS:

A judgment creditor may charge a debtor-partner's interest with payment of any unsatisfied debt. This is **not the judgment creditor's exclusive remedy.**

### 14-9-703

(a) On application to a competent court by a judgment creditor of a partner or of any assignee of a partner, the court may charge the partnership interest of the partner or such assignee with payment of the unsatisfied amount of the judgment, with interest. To the extent so charged, the judgment creditor has only the rights of an assignee of the partnership interest. This chapter shall not deprive any partner of the benefit of any exemption laws applicable to his partnership interest.

(b) **The remedy conferred by this Code section shall not be deemed exclusive of others which may exist**, including, without limitation, the right of a judgment creditor to reach the interest of a partner in the partnership by process of garnishment served on the partnership.

## LIMITED LIABILITY COMPANIES:

A judgment creditor may charge a debtor-member's interest with payment of any unsatisfied debt. This is **not the judgment creditor's exclusive remedy**.

### 14-11-504

(a) On application to a court of competent jurisdiction by any judgment creditor of a member or of any assignee of a member, the court may charge the limited liability company interest of the member or such assignee with payment of the unsatisfied amount of the judgment with interest. To the extent so charged, the judgment creditor has only the rights of an assignee of the limited liability company interest. This chapter does not deprive any member of the benefit of any exemption laws applicable to his or her limited liability company interest.

(b) The remedy conferred by this Code section shall not be deemed exclusive of others which may exist, including, without limitation, the right of a judgment creditor to reach the limited liability company interest of the member by process of garnishment served on the limited liability company.

# Hawaii Judgment Creditor Remedy

## LIMITED PARTNERSHIPS:

Under the Hawaii statues **judicial foreclosure is a remedy**.

### §425E-703 Rights of creditors of partners or transferees

(a) On application to a court of competent jurisdiction by any judgment creditor of a partner or transferee, the court may charge the transferable interest of the judgment debtor with payment of the unsatisfied amount of the judgment with interest. To the extent so charged, the judgment creditor has only the rights of a transferee. The court may appoint a receiver of the share of the distributions due or to become due to the judgment debtor in respect of the partnership and make all other orders, directions, accounts, and inquiries the judgment debtor might have made or which the circumstances of the case may require to give effect to the charging order.

(b) A charging order constitutes a lien on the judgment debtor's transferable interest. **The court may order a foreclosure upon the interest subject to the charging order at any time**. The purchaser at the foreclosure sale has the rights of a transferee.

(c) At any time before foreclosure, an interest charged may be redeemed:

    (1) by the judgment debtor;

    (2) with property other than limited partnership property, by one or more of the other partners; or

    (3) with limited partnership property, by the limited partnership with the consent of all partners whose interests are not so charged.

(d) This chapter shall not deprive any partner or transferee of the benefit of any exemption laws applicable to the partner's or transferee's transferable interest.

(e) This section provides the exclusive remedy by which a judgment creditor of a partner or transferee may satisfy a judgment out of the judgment debtor's transferable interest. [L 2003, c 210, pt of §1]

## LIMITED LIABILITY COMPANIES:

Hawaii statutes provide that the charging order is not the exclusive remedy and specifically **allows for judicial foreclosure** of the member's interest.

### §428-504 Rights of creditors

(a) On application by a judgment creditor of a member of a limited liability company or a member's transferee, a court having jurisdiction may order that the distributional interest of the judgment debtor be used to satisfy the judgment. The court may appoint a receiver to carry out the provisions of the charging order.

(b) A charging order constitutes a lien on the judgment debtor's distributional interest. **The court may order a foreclosure of a lien on a distributional interest subject to the charging order at any time.** A purchaser at the foreclosure sale has the rights of a transferee.

(c) At any time before foreclosure, a distributional interest in a limited liability company which is charged may be redeemed:

    (1) By the judgment debtor;

    (2) With property other than the company's property, by one or more of the other members; or

    (3) With the company's property, but only if permitted by the operating agreement.

(d) This chapter does not affect a member's right under exemption laws with respect to the member's distributional interest in a limited liability company.

(e) This section provides the exclusive remedy by which a judgment creditor of a member or a transferee may satisfy a judgment out of the judgment debtor's distributional interest in a limited liability company.

[L 1996, c 92, pt of §1]

## Idaho Judgment Creditor Remedy

**LIMITED PARTNERSHIPS:**

Idaho statutes provide that the charging order is not the exclusive remedy and specifically **allows for judicial foreclosure** of the partner's interest.

### 53-2-703. Rights of creditor of partner or transferee

(1) On application to a court of competent jurisdiction by any judgment creditor of a partner or transferee, the court may charge the transferable interest of the judgment debtor with payment of the unsatisfied amount of the judgment with interest. To the extent so charged, the judgment creditor has only the rights of a transferee. The court may appoint a receiver of the share of the distributions due or to become due to the judgment debtor in respect of the part-

nership and make all other orders, directions, accounts, and inquiries the judgment debtor might have made or which the circumstances of the case may require to give effect to the charging order.

(2) A charging order constitutes a lien on the judgment debtor's transferable interest. **The court may order a foreclosure upon the interest subject to the charging order at any time.** The purchaser at the foreclosure sale has the rights of a transferee.

(3) At any time before foreclosure, an interest charged may be redeemed:

(a) By the judgment debtor;

(b) With property other than limited partnership property, by one (1) or more of the other partners; or

(c) With limited partnership property, by the limited partnership with the consent of all partners whose interests are not so charged.

(4) This chapter does not deprive any partner or transferee of the benefit of any exemption laws applicable to the partner's or transferee's transferable interest.

(5) This section provides the exclusive remedy by which a judgment creditor of a partner or transferee may satisfy a judgment out of the judgment debtor's transferable interest.

## LIMITED LIABILITY COMPANIES:

Under Idaho statutes the **charging order is the exclusive remedy** until July 1, 2010.

### 53-637. Rights of judgment creditor [Effective until July 1, 2010]. See section 30-6-1104]

On application to a court of competent jurisdiction by any judgment creditor of a member, the court may charge the member's limited liability company interest with payment of the unsatisfied amount of judgment with interest. To the extent so charged, the judgment creditor has only the rights of an assignee of the member's limited liability company interest. **The charging order is the exclusive remedy by which a judgment creditor of the member** or transferee may satisfy a judgment against the member's interest in a limited liability company. The provisions of this chapter do not deprive any member of the benefit of any exemption laws applicable to his limited liability company interest.

# Illinois Judgment Creditor Remedy

## LIMITED PARTNERSHIPS:

Illinois statutes provide that the charging order is not the exclusive remedy and specifically **allows for judicial foreclosure** of the partner's intere

> **Sec. 504 Partner's transferable interest subject to charging order**
>
> (a) On application by a judgment creditor of a partner or of a partner's transferee, a court having jurisdiction may charge the transferable interest of the judgment debtor to satisfy the judgment. The court may appoint a receiver of the share of the distributions due or to become due to the judgment debtor in respect of the partnership and make all other orders, directions, accounts, and inquiries the judgment debtor might have made or which the circumstances of the case may require.
>
> (b) A charging order constitutes a lien on the judgment debtor's transferable interest in the partnership. The court may order a foreclosure of the interest subject to the charging order at any time. The purchaser at the foreclosure sale has the rights of a transferee.
>
> (c) At any time before foreclosure, an interest charged may be redeemed:
>
>   (1) by the judgment debtor;
>
>   (2) with property other than partnership property, by one or more of the other partners; or
>
>   (3) with partnership property, by one or more of the other partners with the consent of all of the partners whose interests are not so charged.
>
> (d) This Act does not deprive a partner of a right under exemption laws with respect to the partner's interest in the partnership.
>
> (e) This Section provides the exclusive remedy by which a judgment creditor of a partner or partner's transferee may satisfy a judgment out of the judgment debtor's transferable interest in the partnership.
>
> (Source: P.A. 92-740, effective 1-1-03.)

## LIMITED LIABILITY COMPANIES:

Illinois statutes provide that the charging order is not the exclusive remedy and specifically **allows for judicial foreclosure** of the debtor member's membership interest.

**Sec. 30-20 Rights of creditor**

(a) On application by a judgment creditor of a member of a limited liability company or of a member's transferee, a court having jurisdiction may charge the distributional interest of the judgment debtor to satisfy the judgment. The court may appoint a receiver of the share of the distributions due or to become due to the judgment debtor and make all other orders, directions, accounts, and inquiries the judgment debtor might have made or which the circumstances may require to give effect to the charging order.
(b) A charging order constitutes a lien on the judgment debtor's distributional interest. The court may order a foreclosure of a lien on a distributional interest subject to the charging order at any time. A purchaser at the foreclosure sale has the rights of a transferee.

(c) At any time before foreclosure, a distributional interest in a limited liability company that is charged may be redeemed:

- (1) by the judgment debtor;
- (2) with property other than the company's property, by one or more of the other members; or
- (3) with the company's property, but only if permitted by the operating agreement.

(d) This Act does not affect a member's right under exemption laws with

respect to the member's distributional interest in a limited liability company.

(e) This Section provides the exclusive remedy by which a judgment creditor of a member or a transferee may satisfy a judgment out of the judgment debtor's distributional interest in a limited liability company.

(Source: P.A. 90-424, effective 1-1-98)

## Indiana Judgment Creditor Remedy

### LIMITED PARTNERSHIPS:

The Indiana limited partnership statute **does not state that charging order is the exclusive remedy** for a judgment creditor of the debtor partner's partnership interest.

**IC 23-16-8-3 Rights of creditor**

Sec. 3. On application to a court by any judgment creditor of a partner, the court may charge the partnership interest of the partner with payment of the unsatisfied amount of the judgment, with interest. To the extent so charged, the judgment creditor has only the rights of an assignee of the partnership interest. This article does not deprive any partner of the benefit of any exemption laws applicable to the partner's partnership interest

*As added by P.L.147-1988, SEC.1.*

## LIMITED LIABILITY COMPANIES:

The Indiana LLC statute **does not state that charging order is the exclusive remedy** for a judgment creditor of the debtor member's membership interest.

### IC 23-18-6-7 Judgment creditors of members; rightsSec. 7.

(a) On application to a court with jurisdiction by a judgment creditor of a member, the court may charge the interest of the member in the limited liability company with the payment of the unsatisfied amount of the judgment with interest.

(b) To the extent the court charges under subsection (a), the judgment creditor has only the rights of an assignee of the member's interest in the limited liability company.

(c) This article does not deprive a member of the benefit of any exemption laws applicable to the member's interest in the limited liability company.

# Iowa Judgment Creditor Remedy

## LIMITED PARTNERSHIPS:

The Iowa limited partnership statute **does not state that charging order is the exclusive remedy** for a judgment creditor of the debtor partner's partnership interest

### 487.703 Rights of creditor

A judgment creditor of a partner may bring an action in the district court charging the partnership interest of the partner with payment of the unsatisfied amount of the judgment. To the extent the court so charges, the judgment creditor has only the rights of an assignee of the partnership interest. This chapter does not deprive a partner of the benefit of exemption laws applicable to the partner's interest.

## LIMITED LIABILITY COMPANIES:

The Iowa LLC statute specifically allows forjudicial foreclosure as a remedy.

### 498.503 Charging order

1. On application by a judgment creditor of a member or transferee, a court may enter a charging order against the transferable interest of the judgment debtor for the unsatisfied amount of the judgment. A charging order constitutes a lien on a judgment debtor's transferable interest and requires the limited liability company to pay over to the person to which the charging order was issued any distribution that would otherwise be paid to the judgment debtor.

2. To the extent necessary to effectuate the collection of distributions pursuant to a charging order in effect under subsection 1, the court may do all of the following:

   a. Appoint a receiver of the distributions subject to the with the power to make all inquiries the judgment debtor might have made.

   b. Make all other orders necessary to give effect to the charging order.

3. Upon a showing that distributions under a charging order will not pay the judgment debt within a reasonable time, the court may foreclose the lien and order the sale of the transferable interest. The purchaser at the foreclosure sale only obtains the transferable interest, does not thereby become a member, and is subject to section 489.502.

4. At any time before foreclosure under subsection 3, the member or transferee whose transferable interest is subject to a charging order under subsection 1 may extinguish the charging order by satisfying the judgment and filing a certified copy of the satisfaction with the court that issued the charging order.

5. At any time before foreclosure under subsection 3, a limited liability company or one or more members whose transferable interests are not subject to the charging order may pay to the judgment creditor the full amount due under the judgment and thereby succeed to the rights of the judgment creditor, including the charging order.

6. This chapter does not deprive any member or transferee of the benefit of any exemption laws applicable to the member's or transferee's transferable interest.

7. This section provides the exclusive remedy by which a person seeking to enforce a judgment against a member or transferee may,

in the capacity of judgment creditor, satisfy the judgment from the judgment debtor's transferable interest.

## Kansas Judgment Creditor Remedy

**LIMITED PARTNERSHIPS:**

The Kansas limited partnership statute **allows for judicial foreclosure** of the debtor partner's partnership interest.

> **56a-504. Partner's transferable interest subject to charging order**
>
> (a) On application by a judgment creditor of a partner or of a partner's transferee, a court having jurisdiction may charge the transferable interest of the judgment debtor to satisfy the judgment. The court may appoint a receiver of the share of the distributions due or to become due to the judgment debtor in respect of the partnership and make all other orders, directions, accounts, and inquiries the judgment debtor might have made or which the circumstances of the case may require.
>
> (b) A charging order constitutes a lien on the judgment debtor's transferable interest in the partnership. The court may order a foreclosure of the interest subject to the charging order at any time. The purchaser at the foreclosure sale has the rights of a transferee.
>
> (c) At any time before foreclosure, an interest charged may be redeemed:
>
> > (1) by the judgment debtor;
> >
> > (2) with property other than partnership property, by one or more of the other partners; or
> >
> > (3) with partnership property, by one or more of the other partners with the consent of all of the partners whose interests are not so charged.
>
> (d) This act does not deprive a partner of a right under exemption laws with respect to the partner's interest in the partnership.
>
> (e) This section provides the exclusive remedy by which a judgment creditor of a partner or partner's transferee may satisfy a judgment out of the judgment debtor's transferable interest in the partnership.
>
> **History:** L. 1998, ch. 93, § 29; Jan. 1, 1999.

## LIMITED LIABILITY COMPANIES:

Under Kansas statutes a judgment credit may receive a charging order on the debtor member's membership interest. **This is the exclusive remedy.**

### 17-76,113. Rights of judgment creditor

On application to a court of competent jurisdiction by any judgment creditor of a member, the court may charge the limited liability company interest of the member with payment of the unsatisfied amount of the judgment with interest. To the extent so charged, the judgment creditor has only the rights of an assignee of the limited liability company interest. This act does not deprive any member of the benefit of any exemption laws applicable to the member's limited liability company interest. **The rights provided by this section to the judgment creditor shall be the sole and exclusive remedy of a judgment creditor with respect to the member's limited liability company interest.**

**History:** L. 1999, ch. 119, § 52; Jan. 1, 2000.

# Kentucky Judgment Creditor Remedy

## LIMITED PARTNERSHIPS:

The Kentucky limited partnership statute **allows for judicial foreclosure** of the debtor partner's partnership interest.

### 362.2-703. Partner's transferable interest subject to charging order

(1) This section provides the exclusive remedy by which the judgment creditor of a partner or the transferee of a partner may satisfy a judgment out the judgment debtor's transferable interest.

(2) On application to a court of competent jurisdiction by any judgment creditor of a partner or a partner's transferee, the court may charge the transferable interest of the judgment debtor with payment of the unsatisfied amount of the judgment. To the extent so charged, the judgment creditor has only the rights of a transferee, and shall have no right to participate in the management or to cause the dissolution of the partnership. The court may appoint a receiver of the share of the distributions due or to become due to the judgment debtor in respect of the partnership and make all other orders, directions, accounts, and inquiries the judgment debtor

might have made or which the circumstances of the case may require to give effect to the charging order.

(3) A charging order constitutes a lien on and the right to receive distributions made with respect to the judgment debtor's transferable interest. A charging order does not of itself constitute an assignment of the transferable interest.

**(4) The court may order a foreclosure upon the transferable interest subject to the charging order at any time.** The purchaser at the foreclosure sale has the rights of a transferee.

(5) At any time before foreclosure, an interest charged may be redeemed:

   (a) by the judgment debtor.
   (b) with property other than limited partnership property, by one (1) or more of the other partners; or
   (c) with limited partnership property, by the limited partnership with the consent of all partners whose interest are not so charged.

(6) This subchapter does not deprive any partner or a partner's transferee of the benefit of any exemption laws applicable to the partner's or transferee's transferable interest.

**Effective:** June 26, 2007

## LIMITED LIABILITY COMPANIES:

The Kentucky LLC statute specifically allows for **judicial foreclosure as a remedy**.

### 1.260 Member's transferable interest subject to charging order

(1) This section provides the exclusive remedy by which the judgment creditor of a member or the transferee of a member may satisfy a judgment out the judgment debtor's transferable interest.

(2) On application to a court of competent jurisdiction by any judgment creditor of a member or a member's transferee, the court may charge the transferable interest of the judgment debtor with payment of the unsatisfied amount of the judgment. To the extent so charged, the judgment creditor has only the rights of a transferee, and shall have no right to participate in the management or to cause the dissolution of the limited liability company. The court may appoint a receiver of the share of the distributions due or to become due to the judgment debtor in respect of the limited liability company

and make all other orders, directions, accounts, and inquiries the judgment debtor might have made or which the circumstances of the case may require to give effect to the charging order.

(3) A charging order constitutes a lien on and the right to receive distributions made with respect to the judgment debtor's transferable interest. A charging order does not of itself constitute an assignment of the transferable interest.

**(4) The court may order a foreclosure upon the transferable interest subject to the charging order at any time.** The purchaser at the foreclosure sale has the rights of a transferee. At any time before foreclosure, an interest charged may be redeemed:

(a) by the judgment debtor.

(b) with property other than limited liability company property, by one or more of the other members; or

(c) with limited liability company property, by the limited liability company with the consent of all members whose interest are not so charged.

(5) This subchapter does not deprive any member or a member's transferee of the benefit of any exemption laws applicable to the member's or transferee's transferable interest.

**Effective:** June 26, 2007

## Louisiana Judgment Creditor Remedy

### LIMITED PARTNERSHIPS:

A charging order is **not the exclusive remedy**.

### LIMITED LIABILITY COMPANIES:

Under the Louisiana statute a **charging order is not the exclusive remedy**.

#### RS 12:1331 Rights of judgment creditor

On application to a court of competent jurisdiction by any judgment creditor of a member, the court may charge the membership interest of the member with payment of the unsatisfied amount of judgment with interest. To the extent so charged, the judgment creditor shall have only the rights of an assignee of the membership interest. This Chapter shall not deprive any member of the benefit of any exemption laws applicable to his membership interest.

Acts 1992, No. 780, §2, effective July 7, 1992

# Maine Judgment Creditor Remedy

**LIMITED PARTNERSHIPS:**

The Maine limited partnership statute **allows for judicial foreclosure** of the debtor partner's partnership interest.

### §1383 Rights of judgment creditor of partner or transferee

1. Court order charging transferable interest; rights of transferee. On application to a court of competent jurisdiction by any judgment creditor of a partner or transferee, the court may charge the transferable interest of the judgment debtor with payment of the unsatisfied amount of the judgment with interest. To the extent so charged, the judgment creditor has only the rights of a transferee. The court may appoint a receiver of the share of the distributions due or to become due to the judgment debtor in respect of the partnership and make all other orders, directions, accounts, and inquiries the judgment debtor might have made or that the circumstances of the case may require to give effect to the charging order.

[ 2005, c. 543, Pt. C, §2 (NEW) ]

2. Charging order a lien; foreclosure; rights of transferee. A charging order constitutes a lien on the judgment debtor's transferable interest. The court may order a foreclosure upon the interest subject to the charging order at any time. The purchaser at the foreclosure sale has the rights of a transferee.

[ 2005, c. 543, Pt. C, §2 (NEW) ]

3. Redemption before foreclosure. At any time before foreclosure, an interest charged may be redeemed:

   (a) by the judgment debtor; [2005, c. 543, Pt. C, §2 (NEW)]

   (b) with property other than limited partnership property, by one or more of the other partners; or [2005, c. 543, Pt. C, §2 (NEW)]

   (c) with limited partnership property, by the limited partnership with the consent of all partners whose interests are not so charged. [2005, c. 543, Pt. C, §2 (NEW).]

[ 2005, c. 543, Pt. C, §2 (NEW).]

4. Exemption laws applicable. This chapter does not deprive any partner or transferee of the benefit of any exemption laws applicable

to the partner's or transferee's transferable interest.

[ 2005, c. 543, Pt. C, §2 (NEW) ]

5. Exclusive remedy. This section provides the exclusive remedy by which a judgment creditor of a partner or transferee may satisfy a judgment out of the judgment debtor's transferable interest.

[ 2005, c. 543, Pt. C, §2 (NEW) ]

## LIMITED LIABILITY COMPANIES:

Under the Maine statute a **charging order is not the exclusive remedy**.

### §686 Rights of judgment creditor

On application to a court of competent jurisdiction by a judgment creditor of a member, the court may charge the membership interest of the member with payment of the unsatisfied amount of judgment with interest. To the extent so charged, the judgment creditor has only the rights of an assignee of the membership interest. This Act does not deprive a member of the benefit of any exemption laws applicable to that member's membership interest. [1993, c. 718, Pt. A, §1 (NEW)]

# Maryland Judgment Creditor Remedy

## LIMITED PARTNERSHIPS:

Under the Maryland statute a **charging order is not the exclusive remedy**.

### §10–705

On application to a court of competent jurisdiction by any judgment creditor of a partner, the court may charge the partnership interest of the partner with payment of the unsatisfied amount of the judgment with interest. To the extent so charged, the judgment creditor has only the rights of an assignee of the partnership interest. This title does not deprive any partner of the benefit of any exemption laws applicable to his partnership interest.

## LIMITED LIABILITY COMPANIES:

Under the Maryland statute a **charging order is not the exclusive remedy**.

**§4A–607**

(a) On application to a court of competent jurisdiction by any judgment creditor of a member, the court may charge the interest of the member in the limited liability company with the payment of the unsatisfied amount of the judgment with interest.

(b) To the extent so charged, the judgment creditor shall have only the rights of an assignee of the member's interest in the limited liability company.

(c) This title does not deprive a member of the benefit of any exemption laws applicable to the member's interest in the limited liability company.

## Massachusetts Judgment Creditor Remedy

### LIMITED PARTNERSHIPS:

Under the Massachusetts statute a **charging order is not the exclusive remedy**.

#### Chapter 109: Section 41 Rights of judgment creditor

Section 41 On application to a court of competent jurisdiction by any judgment creditor of a partner, the court may charge the partnership interest of the partner with payment of the unsatisfied amount of the judgment with interest. To the extent so charged, the judgment creditor has only the rights of an assignee of the partnership interest. This chapter shall not deprive any partner of the benefit of any exemption laws applicable to his partnership interest.

### LIMITED LIABILITY COMPANIES:

Under the Massachusetts statute a **charging order is not the exclusive remedy**.

#### Chapter 156C: Section 40 Judgment against member payable with interest in limited liability company

Section 40 On application to a court of competent jurisdiction by any judgment creditor of a member, the court may charge the limited liability company interest of the member with payment of the unsatisfied amount of the judgment with interest. To the extent so charged, the judgment creditor has only the rights of an assignee of the limited liability company interest. This chapter does not deprive any member of the benefit of any exemption laws applicable to his limited liability company interest.

# Michigan Judgment Creditor Remedy

### LIMITED PARTNERSHIPS:

Under the Michigan statute a **charging order is not the exclusive remedy**.

**449.1703 Charging partnership interest with payment of unsatisfied amount of judgment; rights of judgment creditor; exemptions**

#### Sec. 703

Upon application to a court of competent jurisdiction by any judgment creditor of a partner, the court may charge the partnership interest of the partner with payment of the unsatisfied amount of the judgment with interest. To the extent so charged, the judgment creditor has only the rights of an assignee of the partnership interest. This act does not deprive any partner of the benefit of any exemptions provided by law applicable to his or her partnership interest.

### LIMITED LIABILITY COMPANIES:

Under the Michigan statute a **charging order is not the exclusive remedy**.

**450.4507 Charging membership interest with payment of judgment; rights of judgment creditor; rights and powers of member**

#### Sec. 507

(1) On application to a court of competent jurisdiction by any judgment creditor of a member, the court may charge the membership interest of the member with payment of the unsatisfied amount of judgment with interest. To the extent the membership interest is so charged, the judgment creditor has only the rights of an assignee of the membership interest. This act does not deprive any member of the benefit of any exemption laws applicable to his or her membership interest.

(2) Unless otherwise provided in an operating agreement, the member remains a member and retains all rights and powers of

membership except the right to receive distributions to the extent charged.

# Minnesota Judgment Creditor Remedy

**LIMITED PARTNERSHIPS:**

Under the Minnesota statute **judicialforeclosure is a remedy**.

### 321.0703 Rights of creditor of partner or transferee

(a) On application to a court of competent jurisdiction by any judgment creditor of a partner or transferee, the court may charge the transferable interest of the judgment debtor with payment of the unsatisfied amount of the judgment with interest. To the extent so charged, the judgment creditor has only the rights of a transferee. The court may appoint a receiver of the share of the distributions due or to become due to the judgment debtor in respect of the partnership and make all other orders, directions, accounts, and inquiries the judgment debtor might have made or which the circumstances of the case may require to give effect to the charging orde(b) A charging order constitutes a lien on the judgment debtor's transferable interest. The court may order a foreclosure upon the interest subject to the charging order at any time. The purchaser at the foreclosure sale has the rights of a transferee.

(c) At any time before foreclosure, an interest charged may be redeemed:

(1) by the judgment debtor;

(2) with property other than limited partnership property, by one or more of the other partners; or

(3) with limited partnership property, by the limited partnership with the consent of all partners whose interests are not so charged.

(d) This chapter does not deprive any partner or transferee of the benefit of any exemption laws applicable to the partner's or transferee's transferable interest.

(e) This section provides the exclusive remedy by which a judgment creditor of a partner or transferee may satisfy a judgment out of the judgment debtor's transferable interest.

## LIMITED LIABILITY COMPANIES:

Under Minnesota statutes a judgment credit may receive a charging order on the debtor member's membership interest. **This is the exclusive remedy.**

### 322B.32 Rights of judgment creditor

On application to a court of competent jurisdiction by any judgment creditor of a member, the court may charge a member's or an assignee's financial rights with payment of the unsatisfied amount of the judgment with interest. To the extent so charged, the judgment creditor has only the rights of an assignee of a member's financial rights under section 322B.31. This chapter does not deprive any member or assignee of financial rights of the benefit of any exemption laws applicable to the membership interest. **This section is the sole and exclusive remedy of a judgment creditor with respect to the judgment debtor's membership interest.**

# Mississippi Judgment Creditor Remedy

## LIMITED PARTNERSHIPS:

Under the Mississippi statute **judicial foreclosure is a remedy.**

### SEC. 79-13-504 Partner's transferable interest subject to charging order

(a) On application by a judgment creditor of a partner or of a partner's transferee, a court having jurisdiction may charge the transferable interest of the judgment debtor to satisfy the judgment. The court may appoint a receiver of the share of the distributions due or to become due to the judgment debtor in respect of the partnership and make all other orders, directions, accounts, and inquiries the judgment debtor might have made or which the circumstances of the case may require.

(b) A charging order constitutes a lien on the judgment debtor's transferable interest in the partnership. The court may order a foreclosure of the interest subject to the charging order at any time. The purchaser at the foreclosure sale has the rights of a transferee.

(c) At any time before foreclosure, an interest charged may be redeemed:

    (1) by the judgment debtor;

(2) with property other than partnership property, by one or more of the other partners; or

(3) with partnership property, by one or more of the other partners with the consent of all of the partners whose interests are not so charged.

(d) This act does not deprive a partner of a right under exemption laws with respect to the partner's interest in the partnership.

(e) This section provides the exclusive remedy by which a judgment creditor of a partner or partner's transferee may satisfy a judgment out of the judgment debtor's transferable interest in the partnership.

Sources: Laws, 2004, ch. 458, § 504, SB 2504, effective from and after Jan. 1, 2005

## LIMITED LIABILITY COMPANIES:

Under the Mississippi statute a **charging order is not the exclusive remedy**.

### SEC. 79-29-703 Rights of creditor

On application to a court of competent jurisdiction by a judgment creditor of a member, the court may charge the limited liability company interest of the member with payment of the unsatisfied amount of the judgment, with interest. To the extent so charged, the judgment creditor has only the rights of an assignee of the limited liability company interest. This article does not deprive any member of the benefit of any exemption laws applicable to his limited liability company interest.

**Sources:** Laws, 1994, ch. 402, Sec. 45, effective from and after July 1, 1994

# Missouri Judgment Creditor Remedy

## LIMITED PARTNERSHIPS:

Under the Missouri statute a **charging order is not the exclusive remedy**. However under case law **judicial foreclosure is a remedy**. *Deutsch v. Wolf*, 7 S.W. 3d 460 (Mo. App. 1999)

### Rights of judgment creditor of partner

359.421 On application to a court of competent jurisdiction by any judgment creditor of a partner, the court may charge the partnership interest of the partner with payment of the unsatisfied amount of the judgment with interest. To the extent so charged, the judgment creditor has only the rights of an assignee of the partnership interest. This chapter does not deprive any partner of the benefit of any exemption laws applicable to his partnership interest.

## LIMITED LIABILITY COMPANIES:

Under the Missouri statute a **charging order is not the exclusive remedy**.

### Judgment creditor of member, charge of member's interest with payment of unsatisfied judgment.

347.119 On application to a court of competent jurisdiction by any judgment creditor of a member, the court may charge the member's interest in the limited liability company with payment of the unsatisfied amount of the judgment with interest. To the extent so charged, the judgment creditor has only the rights of an assignee of the member's interest. Sections 347.010 to 347.187 do not deprive any member of the benefit of any exemption laws applicable to his interest in the limited liability company.

# Montana Judgment Creditor Remedy

## LIMITED PARTNERSHIPS:

Under the Montana statute a **charging order is not the exclusive remedy**.

### 35-12-1103 Rights of creditors

On due application to a court of competent jurisdiction by any judgment creditor of a partner, the court may charge the partnership interest of the partner with payment of the unsatisfied amount of the judgment debt, with interest thereon. To the extent so charged, the judgment creditor has only the rights of an assignee of the partnership interest. This chapter does not deprive any partner of the benefit of any exemption laws applicable to his partnership interest.

History: En. Sec. 44, Ch. 522, L. 1981.

## LIMITED LIABILITY COMPANIES:

Under the Montana statute a judicial foreclosure is a remedy.

**35-8-705 Rights of judgment creditor**

(1) On application to a court of competent jurisdiction by any judgment creditor of a member, the court may charge the distributional interest of the member with payment of the unsatisfied amount of judgment, with interest. To the extent charged, the judgment creditor has only the rights of an assignee of the distributional interest. This chapter does not deprive a member of the benefit of any exemption laws applicable to a distributional interest.

(2) The court may appoint a receiver of the share of the distributions due or to become due to a judgment debtor and make all other orders, directions, accounts, and inquiries that the judgment debtor may have made or that the circumstances require to give effect to the charging order.

(3) A charging order constitutes a lien on the judgment debtor's distributional interest. The court may order a foreclosure of a lien on a distributional interest subject to the charging order at any time. A purchaser of the distributional interest at a foreclosure sale has the rights of a transferee.

(4) At any time before foreclosure, a distributional interest that is charged may be redeemed:

    (a) by the judgment debtor;

    (b) by one or more of the other members with property other than the company's; or

    (c) with the company's property if permitted by the operating agreement.

(5) This section provides the exclusive remedy by which a judgment creditor of a member or a transferee may satisfy a judgment out of the judgment debtor's distributional interest in a limited liability company.

History: En. Sec. 42, Ch. 120, L. 1993; amd. Sec. 28, Ch. 302, L. 1999

## Nebraska Judgment Creditor Remedy

**LIMITED PARTNERSHIPS:**

Under the Montana statute a **charging order is not the exclusive remedy**.

**67-273 Rights of judgment creditor of a partner**

    On application to a court of competent jurisdiction by any judgment creditor of a partner, the court may charge the partnership interest of the partner with payment of the unsatisfied amount of the judgment with interest. To the extent so charged, the judgment creditor has only the rights of an assignee of the partnership interest. The Nebraska Uniform Limited Partnership Act does not deprive any partner of the benefit of any exemption laws applicable to his or her partnership interest.

### LIMITED LIABILITY COMPANIES:

The Nebraska LLC statute has no charging order language.

# Nevada Judgment Creditor Remedy

### LIMITED PARTNERSHIPS:

Under the Nevada statute a **charging order is the exclusive remedy**.

#### NRS 88.535 Rights and remedies of creditor of partner

1. On application to a court of competent jurisdiction by any judgment creditor of a partner, the court may charge the partnership interest of the partner with payment of the unsatisfied amount of the judgment with interest. To the extent so charged, the judgment creditor has only the rights of an assignee of the partnership interest.

2. This section:
   (a) provides the exclusive remedy by which a judgment creditor of a partner or an assignee of a partner may satisfy a judgment out of the partnership interest of the judgment debtor.
   (b) does not deprive any partner of the benefit of any exemption laws applicable to his partnership interest.

(Added to NRS by 1985, 1290; A 2001, 1400, 3199; 2003, 3155; 2003, 20th Special Session, 101)

### LIMITED LIABILITY COMPANIES:

Under the Nevada statute a **charging order is the exclusive remedy**.

#### NRS 86.401 Rights and remedies of creditor of member

1. On application to a court of competent jurisdiction by a judgment creditor of a member, the court may charge the member's interest with payment of the unsatisfied amount of the judgment with

interest. To the extent so charged, the judgment creditor has only the rights of an assignee of the member's interest.

2. This section:

(a) provides the exclusive remedy by which a judgment creditor of a member or an assignee of a member may satisfy a judgment out of the member's interest of the judgment debtor.

(b) does not deprive any member of the benefit of any exemption applicable to his interest.

(Added to NRS by 1991, 1302; A 2001, 1393, 3199; 2003, 20th Special Session, 71)

# New Hampshire Judgment Creditor Remedy

### LIMITED PARTNERSHIPS:

Under the New Hampshire statute a **charging order is not the exclusive remedy**.

### Chapter 304-A Uniform Partnership Act

#### 304-A:28 Partner's interest subject to charging order

1. On due application to a superior court by any judgment creditor of a partner, the court may charge the interest of the debtor partner with payment of the unsatisfied amount of such judgment debt with interest thereon; and may then or later appoint a receiver of his share of the profits, and of any other money due or to fall due to him in respect to the partnership, and make all other orders, functions, accounts, and inquiries which the circumstances of the case may require.

2. The interest charged may be redeemed at any time before foreclosure, or in case of a sale being directed by the court may be purchased without thereby causing a dissolution:

(a) with separate property, by any one or more of the partners, or

(b) with partnership property, by any one or more of the partners with the consent of all the partners whose interests are not so charged or sold.

3. Nothing in this chapter shall be held to deprive a partner of his right, if any, under the exemption laws, as regards his interest in the partnership.

## Chapter 304-B Uniform Limited Partnership Act

### 304-B:41 Rights of creditor

On application to a court of competent jurisdiction by any judgment creditor of a partner, the court may charge the partnership interest of the partner with payment of the unsatisfied amount of the judgment with interest. To the extent so charged, the judgment creditor has only the rights of an assignee of the partnership interest. This chapter does not deprive any partner of the benefit of any exemption laws applicable to his partnership interest.

However, under case law **judicial foreclosure is a remedy**.

*Baybank v. Catamount Construction, Inc.*, 693 a.2d 1163 (N.H. 1997) stating that a court may look to the UPA for remedies not mentioned in the ULPA (1976), including the **judicial foreclosure sale** of the limited partnership interest.

## LIMITED LIABILITY COMPANIES:

Under the New Hampshire statute a **charging order is not the exclusive remedy**.

### 304-C:47 Rights of judgment creditor

On application to a court of competent jurisdiction by any judgment creditor of a member, the court may charge the limited liability company interest of the member with payment of the unsatisfied amount of the judgment with interest. To the extent so charged, the judgment creditor has only the rights of an assignee of the limited liability company interest. This chapter does not deprive any member of the benefit of any exemption laws applicable to the member's limited liability company interest.

**Source.** 1993, 313:1, effective July 1, 1993

# New Jersey Judgment Creditor Remedy

## LIMITED PARTNERSHIPS:

Under the New Jersey statute a **charging order is not the exclusive remedy**.

### 42:2A-48 Rights of judgment creditor of a partner

Rights of judgment creditor of a partner. On application to a court of competent jurisdiction by any judgment creditor of a partner, the court may charge the partnership interest of the partner with payment of the unsatisfied amount of the judgment with interest. To the extent so charged, the judgment creditor has only the rights of an assignee of the partnership interest. This chapter does not deprive any partner of the benefit of any exemption laws applicable to his partnership interest.

L. 1983, c. 489, s. 47, effective April 1, 1985

## LIMITED LIABILITY COMPANIES:

Under the New Jersey statute a **charging order is the exclusive remedy**.

### 42:2B-45 Rights of judgment creditor of member

45. On application to a court of competent jurisdiction by any judgment creditor of a member, the court may charge the limited liability company interest of the member with payment of the unsatisfied amount of the judgment with interest. To the extent so charged, the judgment creditor has only the rights of an assignee of the limited liability company interest. An action by a court pursuant to this section does not deprive any member of the benefit of any exemption laws applicable to his limited liability company interest. **A court order charging the limited liability company interest of a member pursuant to this section shall be the sole remedy of a judgment creditor**, who shall have no right under P.L.1993, c.210 (C.42:2B-1 et seq.) or any other State law to interfere with the management or force dissolution of a limited liability company or to seek an order of the court requiring a foreclosure sale of the limited liability company interest. Nothing in this section shall be construed to affect in any way the rights of a judgment creditor of a member under federal bankruptcy or reorganization laws.

L.1993,c.210,s.45; amended 1997, c.139, s.18

# New Mexico Judgment Creditor Remedy

## LIMITED PARTNERSHIPS:

Under the New Mexico statute a judicial foreclosure is a remedy.

### 54-1A-504 Partner's transferable interest subject to charging order

(a) On application by a judgment creditor of a partner or of a partner's transferee, a court having jurisdiction may charge the transferable interest of the judgment debtor to satisfy the judgment. The court may appoint a receiver of the share of the distributions due or to become due to the judgment debtor in respect of the partnership and make all other orders, directions, accounts, and inquiries the judgment debtor might have made or which the circumstances of the case may require.

(b) A charging order constitutes a lien on the judgment debtor's transferable interest in the partnership. **The court may order a foreclosure of the interest subject to the charging order at any time.** The purchaser at the foreclosure sale has the rights of a transferee.

(c) At any time before foreclosure, an interest charged may be redeemed:

(1) by the judgment debtor;

(2) with property other than partnership property, by one or more of the other partners; or

(3) with partnership property, by one or more of the other partners with the consent of all of the partners whose interests are not so charged.

(d) The Uniform Partnership Act (1994) [54-1A-1202 NMSA 1978] does not deprive a partner of a right under exemption laws with respect to the partner's interest in the partnership.

(e) This section provides the exclusive remedy by which a judgment creditor of a partner or partner's transferee may satisfy a judgment out of the judgment debtor's transferable interest in the partnership.

## LIMITED LIABILITY COMPANIES:

Under the New Mexico statute a **charging order is not the exclusive remedy**.

### 53-19-35 Rights of judgment creditor of member

On application to a court by any judgment creditor of a member, the court may charge the interest of the member with payment of the unsatisfied amount of the judgment, with interest. To the extent so charged, the judgment creditor has no more rights than those to which an assignee of the member's limited liability company interest would be entitled under the provisions of Section 32 [53-19-32 NMSA 1978] of the Limited Liability Company Act [Chapter 53, Article 19 NMSA 1978]. That act does not deprive any member of the benefit of any exemption laws applicable to his membership interest.

# New York Judgment Creditor Remedy

## LIMITED PARTNERSHIPS:

Under the New York statute a **judicial foreclosure is a remedy**.

### § 54 Partner's interest subject to charging order

1. On due application to a competent court by any judgment creditor of a partner, the court which entered the judgment, order, or decree, or any other court, may charge the interest of the debtor partner with payment of the unsatisfied amount of such judgment debt with interest thereon. Upon such application or upon the granting of an order attaching the interest of the debtor partner before judgment, the court may then or later appoint a receiver of his share of the profits, and of any other money due or to fall due to him in respect of the partnership, and make all other orders, directions, accounts, and inquiries which the debtor partner might have made, or which the circumstances of the case may require.

2. **The interest charged may be redeemed at any time before foreclosure, or in case of a sale being directed by the court may be purchased without thereby causing a dissolution:**

    (a) with separate property, by any one or more of the partners, or

    (b) with partnership property, by any one or more of the partners with the consent of all the partners whose interests are not so charged or sold.

3. Nothing in this act shall be held to deprive a partner of his right, if any, under the exemption laws, as regards his interest in the partnership.

## LIMITED LIABILITY COMPANIES:

Under the New York statute a **charging order is not the exclusive remedy**.

### § 607 Rights of creditors of members

(a) On application to a court of competent jurisdiction by any judgment creditor of a member, the court may charge the membership interest of the member with payment of the unsatisfied amount of the judgment with interest. To the extent so charged, the judgment creditor has only the rights of an assignee of the membership interest. This chapter does not deprive any member of the benefit of any exemption laws applicable to his or her membership interest.

(b) No creditor of a member shall have any right to obtain possession of, or otherwise exercise legal or equitable remedies with respect to, the property of the limited liability company.

# North Carolina Judgment Creditor Remedy

### LIMITED PARTNERSHIPS:

**Revised Uniform Limited Partnership Act:**

Under the North Carolina Revised Uniform Limited Partnership Act a **charging order is not the exclusive remedy**.

#### § 59-703 Rights of creditor

On application to a court of competent jurisdiction by any judgment creditor of a partner, the court may charge the partnership interest of the partner with payment of the unsatisfied amount of the judgment with interest. The general partners shall have no liability to a partner for payments to a judgment creditor pursuant to this provision. To the extent so charged, the judgment creditor has only the rights of an assignee of the partnership interest. This Article does not deprive any partner of the benefit of any exemption laws applicable to his partnership interest. (1985 (Reg. Sess., 1986), c. 989, s. 2)

### LIMITED LIABILITY COMPANIES:

Under the North Carolina Limited Liability Company Act a **charging order is not the exclusive remedy**.

#### § 57C-5-03 Rights of judgment creditor

On application to a court of competent jurisdiction by any judgment creditor of a member, the court may charge the membership interest of the member with payment of the unsatisfied amount of the judgment with interest. To the extent so charged, the judgment creditor has only the rights of an assignee of the membership interest. This Chapter does not deprive any member of the benefit of any exemption laws applicable to his membership interest. (1993, c. 354, s. 1)

However, under case law, a charging order is the exclusive remedy. Herring v. Keasler, 563, S.E.2d 614 (N.C. App. 2002)

# North Dakota Judgment Creditor Remedy

## LIMITED PARTNERSHIPS:

Under the North Dakota statute a **judicial foreclosure is a remedy**.

### 45-10.2-64 (703) Rights of a creditor of partner or transferee

1. On application to a court of competent jurisdiction creditor of a partner or transferee, the court may charge the transferable interest of the judgment debtor with payment of the unsatisfied amount of the judgment with interest. To the extent so charged, the judgment creditor has only the right of a transferee. The court may appoint a receiver of the share of the distributions due or to become due to the judgment debtor in respect of the partnership and make all other orders, directions, accounts, and inquiries the judgment debtor might have made or which the circumstances of the case may require to give effect to the charging order.

2. A charging order constitutes a lien on the transferable interest of the judgment debtor. **The court may order a foreclosure upon the interest subject to the charging order at any time.** The purchaser at the foreclosure sale has the rights of a transferee.

3. At any time before foreclosure, an interest charged may be redeemed:
    a. by the judgment debt;
    b. with property other than limited partnership property, by one or more of the other partners; or
    c. with limited partnership property, by the limited partnership with the consent of all partners whose interests are not so charged.

4. This chapter does not deprive any partner or transferee of the benefit of any exemption laws applicable to the transferable interest of the partner or transferee.

5. **This section provides the exclusive remedy** by which a judgment creditor of a partner or transferee may satisfy a judgment out of the transferable interest of the judgment debtor.

## LIMITED LIABILITY COMPANIES:

Under the North Dakota statute a **charging order is the exclusive remedy**.

### 45-10.2-64 (703) Rights of a judgment creditor

On application to a court of competent jurisdiction by any judgment creditor of a member, the court may charge a member's or an assignee's financial rights with payment of the unsatisfied amount of the judgment with interest.

1. To the extent so charged, the judgment creditor has only the rights of an assignee of the member's financial rights under section 10-32-31.
2. This chapter does not deprive any member or assignee of financial rights of the benefit of any exemption laws applicable to the membership interest.
3. This section is the sole and exclusive remedy of a judgment creditor with respect to the judgment debtor's membership interest.

## Ohio Judgment Creditor Remedy

### LIMITED PARTNERSHIPS:

Under the Ohio statute a **judicial foreclosure is a remedy**.

#### 1775.27 Partner's interest subject to charging order

Effective January 1, 2010, Chapter 1775 is repealed and no longer governs partnerships. 2008 HB332

(A) On due application to a competent court by any judgment creditor of a partner, the court which entered the judgment, order, or decree, or any other court, may charge the interest of the debtor partner with payment of the unsatisfied amount of such judgment debt with interest thereon; and may then or later appoint a receiver of his share of the profits, and of any other money due or to fall due to him in respect of the partnership, and make all other orders, directions, accounts, and inquiries which the debtor partner might have made, or which the circumstances of the case may require.

(B) **The interest charged may be redeemed at any time before foreclosure**, or in case of a sale being directed by the court may be purchased without thereby causing a dissolution:

(1) with separate property, by any one or more of the partners;

(2) with partnership property, by any one or more of the partners with the consent of all the partners whose interests are not so charged or sold.

Sections 1775.01 to 1775.42, inclusive, of the Revised Code do not deprive a partner of his right, if any, under the exemption laws, as regards his interest in the partnership.

Effective Date: 10-01-1953; 2008 HB332 01-01-2010

## LIMITED LIABILITY COMPANIES:

Under the Ohio statute a **judicial foreclosure is a remedy**.

### 1705.19 Rights of judgment creditor

If any judgment creditor of a member of a limited liability company applies to a court of common pleas to charge the membership interest of the member with payment of the unsatisfied amount of the judgment with interest, the court may so charge the membership interest. **To the extent the membership interest is so charged, the judgment creditor has only the rights of an assignee of the membership interest.** Nothing in this chapter deprives a member of the member's statutory exemption.

Effective Date: 07-01-1994; 10-12-2006

# Oklahoma Judgment Creditor Remedy

## LIMITED PARTNERSHIPS:

Under Oklahoma statutes the **charging order is the exclusive remedy**.

### §54-342 Rights of creditor

On application to a court of competent jurisdiction by any judgment creditor of a partner, the court may charge the partnership interest of the partner with payment of the unsatisfied amount of the judgment with interest. To the extent so charged, the judgment creditor has only the rights of an assignee of the partnership interest. **This section shall be the sole and exclusive remedy of a judgment creditor with respect to the judgment debtor's partnership interest.** This act does not deprive any partner of the benefit of any exemption laws applicable to his or her partnership interest.

Added by Laws 1984, c. 50, § 42, effective Nov. 1, 1984. Amended by Laws 1998, c. 422, § 34, effective Nov. 1, 1998

## LIMITED LIABILITY COMPANIES:

Under Oklahoma statutes the **charging order is the exclusive remedy**.

§18-2034 Judgment creditor - Rights and interests

On application to a court of competent jurisdiction by any judgment creditor of a member, the court may charge the membership interest of the member with payment of the unsatisfied amount of the judgment with interest. To the extent so charged, the judgment creditor has only the rights of an assignee of the membership interest. **A charging order entered by a court pursuant to this section shall in no event be convertible into a membership interest through foreclosure or other action.** This act does not deprive any member of the benefit of any exemption laws applicable to his or her membership interest. **This section shall be the sole and exclusive remedy of a judgment creditor with respect to the judgment debtor's membership interest.**

Added by Laws 1992, c. 148, § 35, effective Sept. 1, 1992. Amended by Laws 1993, c. 366, § 18, effective Sept. 1, 1993; Laws 2004, c. 255, § 46, effective Nov. 1, 2004

# Oregon Judgment Creditor Remedy

## LIMITED PARTNERSHIPS:

Under the Oregon statutes a charging order is **not the exclusive remedy**.

### 70.295 Rights of judgment creditor of partner

On application to a court of competent jurisdiction by any judgment creditor of a partner, the court may charge the partnership interest of the partner with payment of the unsatisfied amount of the judgment with interest. To the extent so charged, the judgment creditor has only the rights of an assignee of the partnership interest. This chapter does not deprive any partner of the benefit of any exemption laws applicable to the partner's partnership interest. [1985 c.677 §42]

## LIMITED LIABILITY COMPANIES:

Under the Oregon statutes a charging order is **not the exclusive remedy**.

### 63.259 Rights of judgment creditor against member

On application to a court of competent jurisdiction by any judgment creditor of a member, the court may charge the membership interest of the member with payment of the unsatisfied amount of the judgment with interest. To the extent so charged, the judgment creditor has only the rights of an assignee of the membership interest. This chapter shall not deprive any member of the benefit of any exemption laws applicable to the member's membership interest. [1993 c.173 §52]

## Pennsylvania Judgment Creditor Remedy

### LIMITED PARTNERSHIPS:

Under the Pennsylvania statue a charging order is the exclusive remedy:

8653. Rights of a creditor

On application to a court of competent jurisdiction by any judgment creditor of a partner, the court may charge the partnership interest of the partner with payment of the unsatisfied amount of the judgment with interest. To the extent so charged, the judgment creditor has only the rights of an assignee of the partnership interest. This chapter does not deprive any partner of the benefit of any exemption laws applicable to his partnership interest.

### LIMITED LIABILITY COMPANIES:

The statue does not contain a charging order provision.

## Rhode Island Judgment Creditor Remedy

### LIMITED PARTNERSHIPS:

Under the Rhode Island statutes a **charging order is not the exclusive remedy**.

**§ 7-13-41 Rights of creditor**

On application to a court of competent jurisdiction by any judgment creditor of a partner, the court may charge the partnership interest of the partner with payment of the unsatisfied amount of the judgment with interest. To the extent charged, the judgment creditor has only the rights of an assignee of the partnership interest. This chapter does not deprive any partner of the benefit of any exemption laws applicable to his or her partnership interest.

**LIMITED LIABILITY COMPANIES:**

Under the Rhode Island statutes a charging order is not the exclusive remedy.

### § 7-16-37 Rights of judgment creditor

On application to a court of competent jurisdiction by any judgment creditor of a member, the court may charge the membership interest of the member with payment of the unsatisfied amount of judgment with interest. To the extent charged, the judgment creditor has only the rights of an assignee of the membership interest. This chapter does not deprive any member of the benefit of any exemption laws applicable to that member's membership interest.

## South Carolina Judgment Creditor Remedy

**LIMITED PARTNERSHIPS:**

Under the South Carolina statute a **charging order is not the exclusive remedy**.

### SECTION 33-42-1230 Rights of creditor

On application to a court of competent jurisdiction by any judgment creditor of a partner, the court may charge the partnership interest of the partner with payment of the unsatisfied amount of the judgment with interest. To the extent so charged, the judgment creditor has only the rights of an assignee of the partnership interest. This chapter does not deprive any partner of the benefit of any exemption laws applicable to his partnership interest.

**LIMITED LIABILITY COMPANIES:**

Under the South Carolina statute a **judicial foreclosure is a remedy**.

### Section 33-44-504 Rights of creditor

(a) On application by a judgment creditor of a member of a limited liability company or of a member's transferee, a court having jurisdiction may charge the distributional interest of the judgment debtor to satisfy the judgment. The court may appoint a receiver of the share of the distributions due or to become due to the judgment debtor and make all other orders, directions, accounts, and inquiries the judgment debtor might have made or which the circumstances may require to give effect to the charging order.

(b) A charging order constitutes a lien on the judgment debtor's distributional interest. **The court may order a foreclosure of a lien on a distributional interest subject to the charging order at any time.** A purchaser at the foreclosure sale has the rights of a transferee.

(c) At any time before foreclosure, a distributional interest in a limited liability company which is charged may be redeemed:

(1) by the judgment debtor;

(2) with property other than the company's property, by one or more of the other members; or

(3) with the company's property, but only if permitted by the operating agreement.

(d) This chapter does not affect a member's right under exemption laws with respect to the member's distributional interest in a limited liability company.

(e) This section provides the exclusive remedy by which a judgment creditor of a member or a transferee may satisfy a judgment out of the judgment debtor's distributional interest in a limited liability company.

## South Dakota Judgment Creditor Remedy

### LIMITED PARTNERSHIPS:

Under the South Dakota statutes a **charging order is the exclusive remedy**.

#### 48-7-703 Rights of judgment creditor—Exclusive remedy

On application to a court of competent jurisdiction by any judgment creditor of a partner, the court may charge the partnership interest of the partner with payment of the unsatisfied amount of the judgment with interest. To the extent so charged, the judgment creditor has only the rights of an assignee of the partnership interest. This chapter does not deprive any partner of the benefit of any exemption laws applicable to the partner's partnership interest.

This section provides the exclusive remedy that a judgment creditor of a general or limited partner or of the general or limited partner's assignee may use to satisfy a judgment out of the judgment debtor's interest in the partnership. No other remedy, including foreclosure on the general or limited partner's partnership interest or a court order for directions, accounts, and inquiries that the debtor, general or limited partner might have made, is available to the judgment creditor attempting to satisfy the judgment out of the judgment debtor's interest in the limited partnership, and no other remedy may be ordered by a court.

**Source:** SL 1986, ch 391, § 703; SL 2007, ch 263, § 1

## LIMITED LIABILITY COMPANIES:

Under the South Dakota statutes a **charging order is the exclusive remedy**.

### 47-34A-504 Rights of creditors

(a) On application by a judgment creditor of a member of a limited liability company or of a member's transferee, **a court having jurisdiction may charge the distributional interest of the judgment debtor to satisfy the judgment**.

(b) A charging order constitutes a lien on the judgment debtor's distributional interest

(c) A distributional interest in a limited liability company which is charged may be redeemed:

    (1) by the judgment debtor;

    (2) with property other than the company's property, by one or more of the other members; or

    (3) with the company's property, but only if permitted by the operating agreement

(d) This chapter does not affect a member's right under exemption laws with respect to the member's distributional interest in a limited liability company.

(e) This section provides the **exclusive remedy** that a judgment creditor of a member's distributional interest or a member's assignee may use to satisfy a judgment out of the judgment debtor's interest in a limited liability company. No other remedy, including foreclosure on the member's distributional interest or a court order for directions, accounts, and inquiries that the debtor, member might have made, is available to the judgment creditor attempting to satisfy the judgment out of the judgment debtor's interest in the limited liability company, and no other remedy may be ordered by a court.

**Source:** SL 1998, ch 272, § 504; SL 2007, ch 262, § 1

# Tennessee Judgment Creditor Remedy

## LIMITED PARTNERSHIPS:

Under the Tennessee statutes judicial foreclosure is a remedy

### 61-1-504 Partner's transferable interest subject to charging order

(a) On application by a judgment creditor of a partner or of a partner's transferee, a court having jurisdiction may charge the transferable interest of the judgment debtor to satisfy the judgment. The court may appoint a receiver of the share of the distributions due or to become due to the judgment debtor in respect of the partnership and make all other orders, directions, accounts, and inquiries the judgment debtor might have made or which the circumstances of the case may require.

(b) A charging order constitutes a lien on the judgment debtor's transferable interest in the partnership. **The court may order a foreclosure of the interest subject to the charging order at any time.** The purchaser at the foreclosure sale has the rights of a transferee.

(c) At any time before foreclosure, an interest charged may be redeemed:

  (1) **b**y the judgment debtor;
  (2) with property other than partnership property, by one (1) or more of the other partners; or
  (3) with partnership property, by one (1) or more of the other partners with the consent of all of the partners whose interests are not so charged.

(d) This chapter does not deprive a partner of a right under exemption laws with respect to the partner's interest in the partnership.

(e) This section provides the exclusive remedy by which a judgment creditor of a partner or partner's transferee may satisfy a judgment out of the judgment debtor's transferable interest in the partnership.

[Acts 2001, ch. 353]

### LIMITED LIABILITY COMPANIES:

Under the Tennessee statutes the charging order is the exclusive remedy.

#### 48-218-105 Rights of judgment creditor

On application to a court of competent jurisdiction by any judgment creditor of a member, the court may charge such person's financial rights with payment of the unsatisfied amount of the judgment with interest. To the extent so charged, the judgment creditor has only the rights of an assignee of such person's financial rights under § 48-218-101. This section does not deprive any member or assignee of financial rights of the benefit of any exemption laws applicable to the membership interest. **This section is the sole and exclusive remedy of a judgment creditor with respect to the judgment debtor's membership interest.**

[Acts 1994, ch. 868, § 1]

## Texas Judgment Creditor Remedy

### LIMITED PARTNERSHIPS:

Under the Texas statutes the **charging order is the exclusive remedy**.

#### Sec. 153.256 PARTNER'S PARTNERSHIP INTEREST SUBJECT TO CHARGING ORDER

(a) On application by a judgment creditor of a partner or of any other owner of a partnership interest, a court having jurisdiction may charge the partnership interest of the judgment debtor to satisfy the judgment.

(b) To the extent that the partnership interest is charged in the manner provided by Subsection (a), the judgment creditor has only the right to receive any distribution to which the judgment debtor would otherwise be entitled in respect of the partnership interest.

(c) A charging order constitutes a lien on the judgment debtor's partnership interest.

(d) **The entry of a charging order is the exclusive remedy** by which a judgment creditor of a partner or of any other owner of a partnership interest may satisfy a judgment out of the judgment debtor's partnership interest.

(e) This section does not deprive a partner or other owner of a partnership interest of a right under exemption laws with respect to the judgment debtor's partnership interest.

(f) A creditor of a partner or of any other owner of a partnership interest does not have the right to obtain possession of, or otherwise exercise legal or equitable remedies with respect to, the property of the limited partnership.

Acts 2003, 78th Leg., ch. 182, Sec. 1, effective Jan. 1, 2006

Amended by: Acts 2007, 80th Leg., R.S., Ch. 688, Sec. 125, effective September 1, 2007

## LIMITED LIABILITY COMPANIES:

Under the Texas statutes the **charging order is the exclusive remedy**.

### Sec. 101.112. Member's Membership Interest Subject to Charging Order.

(a) On application by a judgment creditor of a member of a limited liability company or of any other owner of a membership interest in a limited liability company or of any other owner of a membership interest in a limited liability company, a court having jurisdiction may charge the membership interest of the judgment debtor to satisfy the judgment.

(b) If a court charges a membership interest with payment of a judgment is provided by Subsection (a), the judgment creditor has only the right to receive any distribution to which the judgment debtor would otherwise be entitled in respect of the membership interest.

(c) A charging order constitutes a lien on the judgment debtor's membership interest.

(d) The **entry of a charging order is the exclusive remedy** by which a judgment creditor of a member or of any other owner of a membership interest may satisfy a judgment of the judgment debtor's membership interest.

e) This section may not be construed to deprive a member of a limited liability company or any other owner of a membership interest in a limited liability company the benefit of any exemption laws applicable to the membership interest of the member or owner.

## Utah Judgment Creditor Remedy

### LIMITED PARTNERSHIPS:

Under the Utah statutes **a charging order is not the exclusive remedy**.

#### 48-2a-703 Rights of creditor

On application to a court of competent jurisdiction by any judgment creditor of a partner, the court may charge the partnership interest of the partner with payment of the unsatisfied amount of the judgment with interest. To the extent it is the beneficiary of such a charging order, the judgment creditor has only the rights of an assignee of the partnership interest. This chapter does not deprive any partner of the benefit of any exemption laws applicable to his partnership interest.

### LIMITED LIABILITY COMPANIES:

Under the Utah statutes **judicial foreclosure is a remedy**.

#### 48-2c-1103 Rights of creditor of member

(1) (a) On application to a court of competent jurisdiction by any judgment creditor of a member or of a member's assignee, the court may charge the interest in the company of the member or assignee with payment of the unsatisfied amount of the judgment plus interest.

(b) A court charging the interest of a member or assignee under Subsection (1)(a) may then or later appoint a receiver of the share of distributions due or to become due to the judgment debtor in respect of the interest in the company.

(c) A judgment creditor and receiver under this section shall have only the rights of an assignee.

(d) A court may make all other orders, directions, accounts, and inquiries a judgment debtor might make or that the circumstances of the case may require.

(2) (a) A charging order constitutes a lien on the judgment debtor's interest in the company.

**(b) A court may order a foreclosure of the interest subject to a charging order entered under this section at any time.**

(c) The purchaser at a foreclosure sale under Subsection (2)(b) has only the rights of an assignee if there are other members in the company.

(d) Notwithstanding Subsection (2)(c), if the member whose interest is charged under this section is the sole member of the company when the charging order was entered:

(i) the purchaser at a foreclosure sale acquires all rights of the member, including voting rights; and

(ii) the member is considered to have consented to the admission of the purchaser as a member of the company.

(3) Unless otherwise provided in the articles of organization or operating agreement for the company, at any time before foreclosure an interest charged may be redeemed:

(a) by the judgment debtor;

(b) with property other than company property, by one or more of the other members, or

(c) by the company with the consent of all of the members whose interests are not so charged.

(4) This section does not deprive a member of a right under exemption laws with respect to the member's interest in a company.

(5) This section provides the exclusive remedy by which a judgment creditor of a member or a member's assignee may satisfy a judgment out of the judgment debtor's interest in a company.

(6) No creditor of a member shall have any right to obtain possession of, or otherwise exercise legal or equitable remedies with respect to, the property of the company.

## Vermont Judgment Creditor Remedy

**LIMITED PARTNERSHIPS:**

Under the Vermont statutes a **charging order is not the exclusive remedy**.

### § 3463 Rights of creditor

On application to a court of competent jurisdiction by any judgment creditor of a partner, the court may charge the partnership interest of the partner with payment of the unsatisfied amount of the judgment with interest. To the extent so charged, the judgment creditor has only the rights of an assignee of the partnership interest. This chapter does not deprive any partner of the benefit of any exemption laws applicable to his or her partnership interest. (Added 1997, No. 149 (Adj. Sess.), § 4, effective Jan. 1, 1999)

## LIMITED LIABILITY COMPANIES:

Under the Vermont statutes **judicial foreclosure is a remedy**.

### § 3074 Rights of creditor

(a) On application by a judgment creditor of a member of a limited liability company or of a member's transferee, a court having jurisdiction may charge the distributional interest of the judgment debtor to satisfy the judgment. The court may appoint a receiver of the share of the distributions due or to become due to the judgment debtor and make all other orders, directions, accounts, and inquiries the judgment debtor might have made or which the circumstances may require to give effect to the charging order.

(b) A charging order constitutes a lien on the judgment debtor's distributional interest. **The court may order a foreclosure of a lien on a distributional interest subject to the charging order at any time**. A purchaser at the foreclosure sale has the rights of a transferee.

(c) At any time before foreclosure, a distributional interest charged may be redeemed:

  (1) by the judgment debtor;

  (2) with property other than the limited liability company's property, by one or more of the other members; or

  (3) with the limited liability company's property, but only if permitted by the operating agreement or upon the agreement of all members whose interests are not so charged.

(d) This chapter does not affect a member's right under exemption laws with respect to the member's distributional interest in a limited liability company.

(e) This section provides the exclusive remedy by which a judgment creditor of a member or a transferee may satisfy a judgment out of the judgment debtor's distributional interest in a limited liability company. (Added 1995, No. 179 (Adj. Sess.), § 4)

# Virginia Judgment Creditor Remedy

## LIMITED PARTNERSHIPS:

Under the Virginia statute **charging order is the exclusive remedy**.

### § 50-73.46:1 Partner's transferable interest subject to charging order

A. On application by a judgment creditor of a partner or of a partner's assignee, a court having jurisdiction may charge the transferable interest of the judgment debtor to satisfy the judgment. To the extent so charged, the judgment creditor has only the right to receive any distribution or distributions to which the judgment debtor would otherwise have been entitled in respect of the interest.

B. A charging order constitutes a lien on the judgment debtor's transferable interest in the limited partnership.

C. This chapter does not deprive a partner or a partner's assignee of a right under exemption laws with respect to the judgment debtor's interest in the limited partnership.

D. **The entry of a charging order is the exclusive remedy** by which a judgment creditor of a partner or of a partner's assignee may satisfy a judgment out of the judgment debtor's transferable interest in the limited partnership.

E. No creditor of a partner or of a partner's assignee shall have any right to obtain possession of, or otherwise exercise legal or equitable remedies with respect to, the property of the limited partnership.

(2004, c. 601; 2006, c. 912)

## LIMITED LIABILITY COMPANIES:

Under the Virginia statute **charging order is the exclusive remedy**.

### § 13.1-1041.1 Member's transferable interest subject to charging order

A. On application by a judgment creditor of a member or of a member's assignee, a court having jurisdiction may charge the transferable interest of the judgment debtor to satisfy the judgment. To the extent so charged, the judgment creditor has only the right to receive any distribution or distributions to which the judgment debtor would otherwise have been entitled in respect of the interest.

B. A charging order constitutes a lien on the judgment debtor's transferable interest in the limited liability company.

C. This chapter does not deprive a member or a member's assignee of a right under exemption laws with respect to the judgment debtor's interest in the limited liability company.

D. The entry of a charging order is the exclusive remedy by which a judgment creditor of a member or of a member's assignee may satisfy a judgment out of the judgment debtor's transferable interest in the limited liability company.

E. No creditor of a member or of a member's assignee shall have any right to obtain possession of, or otherwise exercise legal or equitable remedies with respect to, the property of the limited liability company.

(2004, c. 601; 2006, c. 912)

## Washington Judgment Creditor Remedy

### LIMITED PARTNERSHIPS:

Under the Washington statutes a **charging order is not the exclusive remedy**.

#### RCW 25.10.410 Rights of creditor

On application to a court of competent jurisdiction by any judgment creditor of a partner, the court may charge the partnership interest of the partner with payment of the unsatisfied amount of the judgment with interest. To the extent so charged, the judgment creditor has only the rights of an assignee of the partnership interest. This chapter does not deprive any partner of the benefit of any exemption laws applicable to his partnership interest.

[1981 c 51 § 41]

### LIMITED LIABILITY COMPANIES:

Under the Washington **statutes a charging order is not the exclusive remedy**.

#### RCW 25.15.255 Rights of judgment creditor

On application to a court of competent jurisdiction by any judgment creditor of a member, the court may charge the limited liability company interest of the member with payment of the unsatisfied amount of the judgment with interest. To the extent so charged, the judgment creditor has only the rights of an assignee of the limited liability company interest. This chapter does not deprive any member of the benefit of any exemption laws applicable to the member's limited liability company interest.

[1994 c 211 § 703]

# West Virginia Judgment Creditor Remedy

## LIMITED PARTNERSHIPS:

Under the West Virginia statutes a **charging order is not the exclusive remedy**.

### §47-9-41 Rights of creditor

On application to a court of competent jurisdiction by any judgment creditor of a partner, the court may charge the partnership interest of the partner with payment of the unsatisfied amount of the judgment with interest. To the extent so charged, the judgment creditor has only the rights of an assignee of the partnership interest. This article does not deprive any partner of the benefit of any exemption laws applicable to his partnership interest.

## LIMITED LIABILITY COMPANIES:

Under the West Virginia statutes **judicial foreclosure is a remedy**.

### §31B-5-504 Rights of creditor

(a) On application by a judgment creditor of a member of a limited liability company or of a member's transferee, a court having jurisdiction may charge the distributional interest of the judgment debtor to satisfy the judgment. The court may appoint a receiver of the share of the distributions due or to become due to the judgment debtor and make all other orders, directions, accounts, and inquiries the judgment debtor might have made or which the circumstances may require to give effect to the charging order.

(b) A charging order constitutes a lien on the judgment debtor's distributional interest. **The court may order a foreclosure of a lien on a distributional interest subject to the charging order at any time.** A purchaser at the foreclosure sale has the rights of a transferee.

(c) At any time before foreclosure, a distributional interest in a limited liability company which is charged may be redeemed:

(1) by the judgment debtor;

(2) with property other than the company's property, by one or more of the other members; or

(3) with the company's property, but only if permitted by the operating agreement

(d) This chapter does not affect a member's right under exemption laws with respect to the member's distributional interest in a limited liability company.

(e) This section provides the exclusive remedy by which a judgment creditor of a member or a transferee may satisfy a judgment out of the judgment debtor's distributional interest in a limited liability company.

## Wisconsin Judgment Creditor Remedy

### LIMITED PARTNERSHIPS:

Under the Wisconsin statutes a **charging order is not the exclusive remedy**.

#### 179.63 Rights of creditor

On application to the circuit court by any judgment creditor of a partner, the court may charge the partnership interest of the partner with payment of the unsatisfied amount of the judgment with interest. To the extent charged, the judgment creditor has only the rights of an assignee of the partnership interest.

### LIMITED LIABILITY COMPANIES:

Under the Wisconsin statutes a charging order is not the exclusive remedy.

#### 183.0705 Rights of judgment creditor

On application to a court of competent jurisdiction by any judgment creditor of a member, the court may charge the member's limited liability company interest with payment of the unsatisfied amount of the judgment. To the extent so charged, the judgment creditor has only the rights of an assignee of the member's limited liability company interest. This section does not deprive any member of the benefit of any exemption laws applicable to the limited liability company interest.

# Wyoming Judgment Creditor Remedy

## LIMITED PARTNERSHIPS:

Under the Wyoming statutes the **charging order is not the exclusive remedy**.

### 17-14-803 Rights of creditor

On application to a court of competent jurisdiction by any judgment creditor of a partner, the court may charge the partnership interest of the partner with payment of the unsatisfied amount of the judgment with interest. To the extent so charged, the judgment creditor has only the rights of an assignee of the partnership interest. This act does not deprive any partner of the benefit of any exemption laws applicable to his partnership interest.

## LIMITED LIABILITY COMPANIES:

Under the Wyoming statutes the charging order is the exclusive remedy.

### 17-15-145 Rights of creditor

On application to a court of competent jurisdiction by a judgment creditor of a member of a limited liability company or a member's transferee, the court may charge the member's distributional interest in the limited liability company with payment of the unsatisfied amount of the judgment with interest. To the extent so charged, the judgment creditor has only the rights of a transferee of the member's interest as provided in W.S. 17-15-122. **The charging order is the exclusive remedy by which a judgment creditor of the member or transferee may satisfy a judgment against the member's interest in a limited liability company.** This section does not deprive any member of a limited liability company of the benefit of any exemption laws applicable to the member's interest.